NOTHING IS EVERYTHING

THE QUINTESSENTIAL TEACHINGS OF
SRI NISARGADATTA MAHARAJ

MOHAN GAITONDE

NOTHING
IS
EVERYTHING

THE QUINTESSENTIAL TEACHINGS OF
SRI NISARGADATTA MAHARAJ

MOHAN GAITONDE

Nothing is Everything

First Edition: 2014

PUBLISHED BY
ZEN PUBLICATIONS
60, Juhu Supreme Shopping Centre,
Gulmohar Cross Road No. 9, JVPD Scheme,
Juhu, Mumbai 400 049. India.
Tel: +91 22 32408074
eMail: info@zenpublications.com
Website: www.zenpublications.com

Book Design: Red Sky Designs, Mumbai

ISBN 13   978-93-82788-97-3

PRINTED BY
REPRO INDIA LIMITED

Contents

❧

ACKNOWLEDGEMENT

*will be failing in my duties if I do not mention the sole person who was responsible for my meeting Sri Nisargadatta Maharaj. My eldest sister late Smt. Sunanda Ramachandra Prabhu was responsible for taking me to Maharaj, in spite of my trying to avoid it for a couple of years. She made me read His writings to change my reluctance to meet Him. Finally, she had to hold my hand, like a child, and take me to Him. With my first meeting with Maharaj her job was over, as in our first meeting itself, the separation of ages dissolved.

I dedicate this book to Smt. Sunanda, without whose efforts, my life would have lost all its meaning and purpose.

MOHAN GAITONDE

TRANSLATOR'S NOTE

I was very fortunate to have *satsang* of Sri Nisargadatta Maharaj for five years. During 1978-81, I was a translator during evening talks, from 5pm to 6.30 pm everyday.

Maharaj did not expect us to interpret His replies to specific questions from visitors. He insisted on our literal translations without omitting any words. He said, "When a question is asked, the replies come from *Nirvikalpa* (a state free of ideation). The replies will have proper impact on the questioner, only if there is literal translation of these (Maharaj's) words. Maharaj was very strict in this matter.

For Maharaj, every visitor was the same as He was. He wondered to see the havoc played by mere imagination and concepts. Just as one would like to wake up anybody troubled by dreams, Maharaj showed deep and earnest efforts to blast concepts for real awakening. All spiritual seekers appreciated His relentless passion for sharing His Real understanding.

Unlike morning sessions, in the evenings there were less questions from visitors. Perhaps, visitors took rest in the evenings and enjoyed hearing Maharaj speaking on His own. After beginning the talks, Maharaj used to invite questions, in case of any doubts. The new comers, if any, would begin with their questions.

When Maharaj talked for a long time, say five minutes or more at a stretch, it was difficult to translate every word in His presence. The same talks are now available on the cassette for word to word translation, without missing anything. In the books edited by the American writers, there is total reliance on the English translations, which are incomplete. Readers may find this translation interesting and useful.

We cannot expect a new skeptical reader to accept this material unconditionally; but if it helps to provoke his serious thoughts, it would be a major achievement.

There are many repetitions in this book, which have been retained, as they are needed for awakening from the deep slumber of ignorance.

Maharaj warned His disciples not to be content with mere knowledge of words, which enabled them to be prominent in spiritual discussions. Almost every day He emphasized the importance of meditation on "I Am" without words, which was a self-revealing process, leading to Self-knowledge.

The content of this book is from the recordings of the conversations in the evenings only. These talks were not recorded with an idea to write a book. The main idea for the recordings, was to have a continued *satsang* of Maharaj, even after His *Maha Samadhi*. That purpose has served so far and will continue till end.

Even after reading almost all the books on Maharaj's talks published so far, I find some portion of these evening recordings absolutely new and ever fresh for all spiritual readers. Hence, this new publication.

I thank Dr. N.Vanaja for arranging for a tape recorder to record these talks and my wife Jayashri for operating the machine economically, every evening.

MOHAN GAITONDE

INTRODUCTION

✦

It is truly an honor to be asked by Mohan and Jayashree Gaitonde, (Maharaj's evening translators) to write an introduction to these recorded dialogues of *Sri Nisargadatta Maharaj* entitled *'Nothing is Everything'*.

Sri Nisargadatta Maharaj paraphrased: Stay at the brink, the space where beingness becomes no-being and no-being becomes being.

As with all of Maharaj's disciples I have ever met, words fail to describe their reverence, devotion and gratitude to their beloved Guru Nisargadatta Maharaj.

For almost 35 years the impact of "His" teachings have flooded and continue to overwhelm "my illusory existence" with their directness, precision, and ability to both point to, and describe **THAT** which is indescribable in words.

As a Guru and spiritual mentor *Nisargadatta Maharaj* changed and shaped the entire course of everyone he touched. I must admit quite frankly, that upon meeting him I had not suspected nor could I even imagine the extraordinary impact, the time I spent with Him, would catalyze and bring about. To paraphrase Maharaj:

The words of a realized man cannot go to waste, they are like seeds, they will wait to the proper time to sprout, but once implanted they will bear their fruit.

In writing an Introduction to Maharaj's teachings, I am reminded of Jean Dunn, (one of Maharaj's closest Western disciples), when she remarked:

"Every sentence Maharaj spoke was like an Upanishad".
Before I proceed with an attempt to describe Maharaj's teaching "style" and his teachings in a brief and concise manner, first let me relate an interaction I had with him. Hopefully this dialogue might help to provide a window into who He really was, where He was coming from, and the teachings which appeared "through Him".

To begin with I, like most others, took Maharaj to be a person an "enlightened" being, and hence treated him and saw him as such.

I soon came to appreciate Maharaj was neither a person nor an "enlightened" being.

To illustrate, one day in the late 1970's I asked Him a question.

Maharaj replied, (Very Intensely!!!):

"You think you are a person so you think Maharaj is a person. You think you are an entity or a deity and so you think Maharaj is an entity or a deity. Maharaj is not a person or an entity or a deity.

Maharaj is Cosmic Consciousness!

I can only say that this "experience" shifted "my consciousness" and enabled me to grasp what was appearing to occur. Appreciating that Maharaj was not a person, an entity or a deity, but ***Cosmic Consciousness itself*** might help to illuminate the teachings and teacher that appeared to occur in this little room on Khetwadi near Grant Road in Bombay,

(Mumbai) for close to 45 years.

Nisargadatta Maharaj, paraphrased: You think I am a person and you are a person conversing with each other. Actually there is only consciousness.

THE UNIQUENESS OF MAHARAJ

The question was what had made Nisargadatta Maharaj so different from any other Guru or teacher I had ever encountered?

To begin with, in my initial meeting with him I actually could not find him in the room. Why? Because with all the Guru's I had met the "energy" seemed to pour from a specific point in the space-time. With Maharaj there was an enormous amount of "energy", a magnetic power which drew me to His presence, but the "energy" did not feel like it came off or from Him personally. Moreover He looked so ordinary. He was dressed not in white robes with a long beard or all in orange with a shaved head. Rather, He dressed and looked like everyone else in His neighborhood. Without drawing attention to his person, (as He often said, "You are not a person", or "there is no person") "He" was just sitting on the floor smoking a *beedi*, (thin Indian cigarette rolled in a *tendu* leaf). There was no spiritual game, no pretense, no hierarchy, no organization and absolutely no game at all.

He once said,

"I am not here to accumulate students."

Paradoxically the overall effect was that of being drawn magnetically to "Him". His "way of being", *(bhaav)* left me in awe with a deep sense of reverence as I tried to "take in" and absorb every word He said.

Another thing that made Maharaj so unique was that "He" never asked anything from me, wanted anything from me, and in a word, He never **needed** anything from me. He was totally student, devotee or disciple centered, not Guru centered. Nor did He try to get me to fit into any model, role, or belief system. It was because of all this that He was totally trustworthy as I knew He was always *"on my side"*.

Another unique ascpect of Maharaj was that He reignited kindling my initial understanding of "spirituality", as **"Finding out who you are"**. And although that was always at the core of my wishes and understanding, I had been sidetracked into believing in cultural and spiritual mythologies and seduced into believing in the "spiritual game". Subtly that had lead me away from *"Finding out who I am"*, and *"going in"*, and got me more into *"fitting in"*.

Another aspect of Maharaj was His extraordinary directness, and confrontational teaching style. Because Maharaj did not need or want anything from you, nor did He need you to come back to start a center or be part of an organization with a mission, He was free to be direct and blunt. His teaching style was so direct that often times the "pain" (as he confronted my most sacred unquestioned concepts) was overwhelming, **but** simultaneously extraordinarily clarifying, emptying, freeing and in a word **liberating**.

If you asked a question you either got a clear and direct answer, or I got a question; **"An Enquiry Question"** which drove me "deeper". His questioning my question pointing and focusing with a Zen Koan type of lazer beam which both absorbed my attention and deconstructed my concepts.

Nisargadatta Maharaj: "This faith in the "I Am', on what does it depend... this faith and belief that you are, on what does it depend upon?"

With such intense focus the enquiry He had proposed if "taken in" and contemplated not only dissolved the question but the answer was revealed from "within". More strikingly soon the question, the answer, and the "I" you thought you were who had asked the question in the first place had dissolved into nothingness.

"My words if implanted in you will destroy all other words and concepts." Nisargadatta Maharaj

As an aside, I had had a misconception having been with many Gurus in the past. I had mistakenly fantasized that if you were "Realized" that somehow you could "teach", convey and transmit teachings. I came to understand that this was not true. I recognized there was no correlation between "Realization" and the ability to teach. What was so extraordinary and liberating was that Maharaj had both the ability to teach and 'Realization', which I soon learned, was very rare.

This happening-teaching was overwhelmingly powerful. Maharaj met each student, "where they were". Like a true "Teaching Master" letting go of His cultural metaphors He translated His cultural metaphors and pointers to fit the person asking the question. For a Westerner this made the transmission of teachings seamless and an ecstatic experience as it was like light bulbs going off "inside" as the concepts held so dear fell away and the empty-ness-fullness was revealed.

Then with great "force of intention" He got seekers to move beyond and let go of their concepts of who and what they were. In this way the intensity of His answers and enquiry focused questions dislodged us from any state we were in, or imagined we were in.

The wonder of Maharaj was that it was this combination

of "Realization, and ability to teach which pointed directly to whatever "path" or "portal" that was a perfect fit for "you", which would unlock "your" door. In other words many teachers presented a one-size-fits-all spiritual practice, *(sadhana)* or prescription or formula which was the same for each student or devotee. Somehow, Maharaj gave answers that were tailor-made to the questioner. And, it was precisely because He did not need or want anything from you that His directness, clarity and integrity went into you like a virus dismantling your concepts as well as the "I" which believed it had concepts.

"I want to blast all your concepts and put you in the no concept state." – Nisargadatta Maharaj

THE TEACHINGS

The teachings of Sri Nisargadatta Maharaj were from a distance quite simple.

The very very brief overall context was:

Advaita, (Sanskrit for not two, or, one substance not two). Ultimately of course there was not one.

and

Vedanta, (*Neti Neti,* Sanskrit for Not this, Not this). Discard everything (termed in Sanskrit *nama-rupa,* names and forms) as Not this, Not this.)
This was the genral context along with:

Find out, who you are?

Stay in the I Am, let go of everything else, or hold onto the I Am and let go of everything else.

Anything you think you are, you are not.

Nisargadatta Maharaj paraphrased: In order to find out who you are, you must first find out who you are not.

BEYOND THE I AM

When a student asked Maharaj, "Who are you?", Maharaj replied, *"Nothing perceivable or conceivable."*

In other words if you can perceive it or conceive it, it was not you, therefore discard it.

For those who were there to understand and gather more "spiritual" information, (spiritual concepts) he said,

"If you can forget it or remember it, it is not you therefore discard it."

Simply stated, discard all perceivable and conceivable as *Not this, Not this.*

And

"Stay in the consciousness as a portal to the Absolute".

At first blush this seemed simple. Metaphorically like peeling an onion until nothing is left as the mind begins to unpack itself. Or, like pulling a string and thread in a ball of yarn. By finding the organizing string and pulling it, the ball of yarn would unravel. In the same way Maharaj would direct "your" attention to "your" concepts or state "you" were in and thereby bring about the unravelling of the mind and its most cherished concepts, *(and believe me Maharaj knew how to pull your string!!!).*

THE ABSOLUTE

What made Maharaj even more unique was that he spoke of the **Absolute**, a state prior to the *I Am* and *consciousness*, and, that basically the *I Am* and *consciousness* was not it, ergo His on-going statement which He repeated again and again and again:

"Prior to Consciousness".
"This "understanding was far beyond anything I had heard or read about at that time.

(*Admittedly Prior to Consciousness* was not clear to me in the 1970's. But much later to realize you can only see and understand through or with the state of consciousness you imagine you are in or are at. In other words it is the lens formed by concepts through which an "I" imagines it is seeing or understanding. The imaginary "I" can only see and understand through that imaginary lens of ideas, i.e. thoughts, memory, emotions, associations, perceptions etc. In this way the "I" (the illusion of there being an "I") can only see its own illusions. For this reason the illusory "I" can only appreciate Maharaj from who and what it imagined it was, and therefore who or what the "I" imagined Maharaj was.

Simply put it I say the word emptiness, one might imagine or have a picture or experience of emptiness like outer space BUT the picture of emptiness or space is not the thing it represents. In short Maharaj was beyond anything "I" could perceive or conceive. On my last visit to Mumbai in 2007 one of Maharaj's long time disciples said, "How could we understand Him, He was way beyond us."

Nisargadatta Maharaj: "Everything you understand, you can only understand through your concepts."

To reiterate once again Maharaj's teaching style was uncompromising, relentless, persistent, and tenacious. He stayed on point, never distracted, hammering home that all perceivables and conceivables were dependent on the belief that You Are or I Am. Ultimately upon the I Am dissolving naturally, as Maharaj said, "You Are not". In this way, there was an apperance of questions being answered, but who was answering the questions?

Nisargadatta Maharaj: "In the absolute state I do not even know that I am."

These interactions with Him were so monumental that even today their directness remain indescribable leaving me breathless, empty and in awe. As you can imagine it is very difficult to summarize His teaching style and teachings in such a short introduction.

So I hope you appreciate this is only a little attempt. "My" interpretation. A tip of the iceberg, a view, a window, written from just one of His disciples. This offering is merely a slice, a tiny description into an unparalleled voice of **Nisargadatta Maharaj, a Voice of That Which Isn't.**

Maybe the best way to conclude is to recall a time when He began pacing and shouting at me:

"There is no birth
There is no death
There is no person
It's all a concept
It's all an illusion!!!!!

As He directed this powerful energetic focus at me, "light" passed from His hand and through "me".

The memory of that day remains with me more than 33

years later.

> May these teachings find a home in your heart.
> With reverence and love for my
> Guru Sri Nisargadatta Maharaj
> *Pranams*
> *Nisargadatta Maharaj Ki Jai!*

July 11, 2012   Stephen H. Wolinsky
                                                Aptos, California

FOREWORD

✤

Jai Guru...

This book is a live *satsang* with Satguru Sri Nisargadatta
Maharaj. And why will it not be when Maharaj's evening
translator Mr Mohan Gaitonde who had the privilege of being
with Maharaj from 1979 to 1981 has transcribed these rare
and unpublished conversations with Sri Nisargadatta through
this book. This book has special importance in the sense that
Mr Gaitonde being well-versed with Marathi, the language
Maharaj spoke, makes it easier for the reader to uncover the real
meaning of Maharaj's words of wisdom. And beloved Guru-
brother Dr Stephen Wolinsky, who too had the opportunity of
satsang with Maharaj, has kindly shared his introduction to
Maharaj's teachings for the benefit of the next generation of
seekers of Truth.

It has been my privilege to interact with both Mr Gaitonde
and Dr Wolinsky and I thank Mr Mohan and Mrs Jayashree
Gaitonde for offering me an opportunity to write this foreword.
It is my pleasure to share my gratitude for Satguru Nisargadatta
Maharaj through this foreword.

Satguru's words have the potency to awaken and eradicate
the disease permanently; if pondered upon, ruminated upon.

Nisargadatta Maharaj says, "For the earnest seeker, liberation is possible just by listening to this knowledge." And that is what happened with Nisargadatta Maharaj too after meeting his Guru Sri *Siddha*rameshwar Maharaj in 1933.

All those who have already arrived HOME, would certainly not be reading this book. As someone without a disease is most unlikely to visit the doctor for treatment and someone who has already graduated is less likely to apply for school admission.

This book is for all those ardent seekers who are in search of the Truth and for those who have been taking medicines from Nisargadatta Maharaj for a longtime. But what is the purpose of any of these medicines? Is it to just accumulate medicines in multitude or is it to get rid off the disease and the medicine forever? When I see or meet people who have been reading Nisargadatta Maharaj's books for years, taking pride in their 'loyalty' towards reading these books, I feel the deepest empathy. For, how long can one keep on taking the medicines? I often feel that some link is missing within the seeker himself.

Through this book, Nisargadatta Maharaj is offering 'The Ultimate Medicine' once again, though on a different platter. In my view Nisargadatta has been describing the effects of medicine rather than offering any prescriptions and expects the fervent seeker to intuitively discriminate and realize by continuous reflection and contemplation on it. But the question arises, is mere contemplation over words of highest wisdom self sufficient?

Although we have seen the highest teachings from Nisargadatta Maharaj through various conversations so far, the fact that how did Nisargadatta 'realize' in such a short span of three years after meeting his Guru, remains ignored! The path that Nisargadatta travelled still remains in the dark. The wisdom that is revealed through Nisargadatta Maharaj is not only through his own contemplation but also through His devotion, dedication and surrender towards His Guru and his teachings. Apart from His earnestness and eagerness, His undeniable faith in His Guru remains ignored, which in fact acted as a natural enzyme to digest the wisdom shared by His Guru and in effect realize His Real Self. I am sure a keen seeker will definitely absorb this pointer.

Often, I am surprised to see the presence of confusion and absence of clarity in the seekers, despite being a regular reader of Maharaj's teachings and in spite of the directness of His utterances. I feel the devoted readers can ponder over a couple of things before reading this book. First, 'Who' is Nisargadatta talking to? And 'Who' is reading or listening to Nisargadatta? For Nisargadatta has been saying relentlessly, "I am talking to the consciousness and not to the body-mind." The seeker, who will read this book with this pointer, will definitely be transcended beyond any reading and beyond any need, which is the whole and sole purpose of Maharaj's teaching.

Nothing is Everything. Someone may ask, how is it possible? Isn't everyone wasting time in search of 'something'? Why so? It could be, because each one assumes him/herself as 'somebody'. But it's never about finding something by somebody. In fact one's assumption and conviction that he/she is merely a body, is the primary obstacle in realizing who they are in reality. This very moment is pregnant and ready to deliver Everything, when you are ready to accept Nothing !

Somehow the word 'Nothing' doesn't interest the seeker whereas the word 'Everything' overwhelms him/her. Why is it so? Why is there so much fear for this 'Nothing'? The thought of one's absence, even though momentary, seems to create fear of non-existence although each and everyone enjoys this absence of 'separate self' every night during deep sleep. The fear of Nothing is fear of death which is in turn the fear of Unknown. The inability to recognize the hidden secret beneath this Nothing, somehow forces the seeker to shut the doors of Ultimate Understanding sans seeker. In short the word Nothing repels and the word Everything attracts him/her, as these apparent contradictions are perceived at their face value. These contradictions do not exist outwardly but rather exist as the inner division in seeker's mind.

May Nisargadatta Maharaj shower blessings on the dedicated seekers in order to gather courage to face the ultimate and divine paradox of Nothing is Everything.

If you are really ready for Nothing, this book is a perfect touchstone. This book which is focussed on Nisargadatta Maharaj's final teachings will surely transcend the seeking into Understanding of who you are by ceasing the seeking forever.

It is such pleasure to present this pristine bouquet of pointers from Satguru Sri Nisargadatta Maharaj to all of you. THAT, the eternal state where, nothing is missing and nothing more is needed. Neither the experience of study nor study of the experience can reveal THAT. THAT is prior and beyond both. The divine light that permanently deletes the notional distance of darkness between you and Your Real Self is Satguru. Nothing can compete with the Grace of Satguru.

Satguru Sharan
With love,

NITIN RAM
Author of 'Self Calling: Self Reminder Meditations'

Seeking or Understanding?

Seeking is based on some reason,
Understanding is without any!

Seeking is with an effort and purpose,
Understanding is spontaneous and effortless!

Understanding is absent in Seeking,
While the 'seeker' is absent in the Understanding!

Seeking consists of seeker, seeking and the sought,
While this trinity is utterly absent in the Understanding!

Search consists of search, searcher and the searched,
Understanding denies the very 'searcher'!

Seeking consists of stages, intervals and may be some practices,
While the Understanding is eternal and despite of them!

Seeking has an aim,
While nature of Understanding is itself aim-less!

Seeking is supported by listening, reading or pondering,
While Understanding is Self-sustaining (Independent)!

Fear of forgetting gathered knowledge prevails in Seeking,
While even the thought of having understood is
absent in Understanding!

Background of Seeking is duality,
While Understanding is groundless Non-Duality!

Seeking is an ever changing state,
Whereas Understanding, a 'stateless' state!

In Seeking, lock exists and search for the key happens,
While in Understanding, clear conviction prevails that
lock and key were never separate!

Jai Guru
NITIN RAM

❧

November 26, 1979

WHY IS LIFE FULL OF STRIFE?

✤

Visitor: I am asking you questions and you are replying. For you, it seems, all these are unimportant questions. May I know what is of importance to you?

Maharaj: In your worldly experience, what is the most important ?

V: I do not know.

M: You came to know that you are, that you exist. What is of more importance to you than the fact that you are? The most important thing is your beingness or consciousness. But that "I Am" ness is the quality of your food body. As long as the consciousness is present, you may acquire worldly knowledge and be proud of it. However, all that will last only until the food juices in the body are wet. When the juices get dried up, the Vasudeva, or the one who smells his beingness will vanish.

V: My so called existence depends upon food juices.

M: When you return to your country, people will ask you, "What knowledge did you gather there?" What would be your reply?

(Silence)

M: All this is name sake *knowledge* or *jnana* (which is correctly pronounced as *dnyana*) Beyond it is *Vijnana* or *Parabrahman*. The unmanifest has manifested with the happening of the child consciousness or the individual soul.

V: Am I that Child.

M: When you are here, talk only about your own experience. Is it not your child consciousness that is responsible for your knowledge of your world? If that child consciousness had not appeared, would you have asked any questions now?

(No reply)

M: In the beginning the consciousness appears, which is like space and with self-love. It is love to exist. Whoever may come here and however scholarly, I know what has come and I catch hold of it. Without that neither he or nor I would talk.

V: Is it possible to change the child consciousness into adult consciousness?

M: It is like asking how to increase the space. Demolish buildings and the space will increase. Beingness is the quality of the food juices. When they vanish, the beingness goes into the no being state. The child consciousness is not knowledge but ignorance. Prior to consciousness, there is no knowledge of 'I Am'. That is transcending knowledge or *Vijnana* or *Parabrahman*. From this unmanifest non-being state appears the child consciousness. How can it be knowledge? Consciousness is material knowledge, as it is the quality of *sattva* or food juices. Without *sattva*, the consciousness cannot appear.

V: Am I not lucky that I was born? Is not consciousness a blessing?

M: It is the greatest blunder for the beingness to appear from the non-being state.

V: Do you suggest that couples should not procreate?

M: *(In English)* : Look at you.

V: Why is life full of strife?

M: You must have noticed the strife amongst the five elements. That strife ultimately settles on the earth. Every grain of rice, wheat etc. is composed of the five elements. This strife goes into your food material. All living beings share this food and with it, the strife.

Just as one is affected by consuming alcohol, one is also affected by the strife in one's food.

❧

November 27, 1979

WHAT IS MEDITATION?

Maharaj: Our sense of being is without a body. It is called *Brahman*. Without your knowledge, the chant of "*I am Brahman*" goes on within you.

One who realizes one's true identity as *Brahman*, is worshipped by spiritual aspirants.

That *Brahman* or God is your true form. This identity has no death. You have fear of death because of your body identity. If you develop your faith as you are told now, you will never experience death. Then you will find no need to ask anybody regarding spiritual matters. Instead, people will visit you in quest of Truth.

Visitor: What is meditation?

M: Not to lose sight of your true identity is meditation. Your body identity should find no room in your faith. When you realize your consciousness as God of all Gods, you will find yourself as infinite and boundless.

V: Is not God greater than me?

M: Your consciousness is the proof that the God is. Without you, who is there to recognise His greatness? Do not forget this fact.

The knower of consciousness has no death. He drops his body in a blissful state.

V: In our world, we have pleasure of achievements.

M: But the risk and fear of failure accompany it. The worst fear is of death.

It is said that the hidden treasures are protected by ghosts of serpents. You have to please the ghosts by suitable offering, before touching the treasure. Improper handling can lead to your death.

Similarly, for Self-knowledge, you have to make offering of your body identity. Thereafter, the Self is free of the body. Then, end of the body becomes blissful.

V: Will chanting "I am not this body" help?

M: You have to be as you are in reality. You are the consciousness and not a man or a woman. You are the knower of light. You can judge its clarity and not the vice versa.

V: What is the influence of *Maya* or the illusion?

M: *Maya* has given you your body form. But when you meet your Sadguru, he gives you your form of consciousness. Initially you were the knower of the body, which has changed to the knower of consciousness. That state is called *Vijnana* or *Parabrahman*.

V: Is it beyond manifestation?

M: The manifestation is due to five elements. As long as you are a part of it, there is bodily suffering. The disciple who sees his Guru as infinite, realizes the same as his form. Seeing his Guru as *Paramatma* the disciple realizes It as himself.

V: What happens to the knowledge of the *Jnani*?

M: The knowledge dissolves or merges into the *Jnani*. The *Jnani* does not dissolve. The states of waking and sleep are absent in a *Jnani*. He has no name and form. All these remain upto Self-knowledge, but not beyond. All this is very easy, but it appears to be very difficult of comprehension. A rare one can realize it. One has to transcend not only the body, but even one's consciousness. One goes beyond all knowledge. All these changes happen without any deliberate rejection of the old identities.

Like a vast overrolling mass of water, from the supreme consciousness, the consciousness comes into existence. *Purusha* is cosmic spirit, *Pura* meaning flood. *Purusha* is only a witness. All activities are due to *Yoga-maya* or the *yogic* illusion.

Uninvited, she takes the forms to act. The real actions are due to the vital breath, which is due to the five elements. The five elements, three *gunas* (*sattva*, *rajas* and *tamas*), and *Prakriti*, *Purusha* add up to the figure of ten. These are my organs of knowledge and action. Due to the *sattva* or food essence, the consciousness appears and all the suffering is due to this consciousness. All this happening and the experience due to consciousness is uncalled for and extravagant. I have no part in all this happening.

V: Can you describe your state, so that I can understand it?

M: The words cannot describe Me. The words and their meaning are totally inadequate for That. You are also the same.

V: Then, how this body identity?

M: When did this identity come?

V: I do not remember. But it is bound to be after my birth.

M: Were you present at the time of your birth?

V: As I was born and my birth was celebrated by my parents, I must have been present there.

M: So, that is not your knowledge, but only an inference.

V: Quite so.

M: Try to recollect the earliest incident in your life. How old were you, then?

V: I remember my visit to Niagara, when I was four years old.

M: That is the beginning of your identity. Around that age, you must have recognized your mother. She told you your name as Wilson and that you were a boy and not a girl.

V: If I were *Paramatma*, I should have known about myself without my mother telling me that.

M: *Paramatma* is in a state of non-being. It is similar to your deep sleep experience.

V: Is He always in deep sleep?

M: He never sleeps; hence the term waking also does not apply to Him.

V: It is very interesting. Please tell me more about That.

M: At the time of your conception in your mother's womb, it was the beginning of the manifestation. Prior to that you were unmanifest and in the non-being state. After conception the non-being state continued. Your manifestation is similar to the sudden appearance of light by striking a match stick. There is only light- there is nothing before it and nothing after it. Your identity with name and form started functioning from your age of four. As your appearance is from a non-being state, you had to begin your knowledge from zero. You did not know what you were. The nearest to you was your body. Naturally, you felt that you were the body and your mother and others confirmed it. It could also be the vice versa i.e. your mother told you that you were the body and its name Wilson. You had no choice but to put your stamp of confirmation on it.

After the appearance of the living form, *Paramatma* accepts the name and form and adjusts to what is happening around. What is happening and why, He does not know.

The whole life of the form is like a lighted matchstick and it continues as long as the light lasts. Do the five elements have a form?

V: No.

M: There is no creator for all this. It is all a spontaneous happening.

Everything is fine until the forms appear with the beingness, with self-love- the love to be. With life, the struggle to survive begins. All the activities of all living beings is to sustain the beingness. This involves protection of their bodies and searching for food. Other than this they have no knowledge of their origin. The cosmic substance and the cosmic spirit are bodiless; but all living bodies come into existence because of them. All this worldly show is uncalled for, without any need for it. I say that my body is the union of the five elements. This applies to all forms including yours. You know it. Your body occupies space, which is its part. There is air in it. The body temperature shows the presence of heat. The major portion of the body is water and all the remaining content is from the earth. The whole body is the food of the consciousness, which is the quality of food essence.

In the whole existence, the suffering is only due to consciousness.

V: It is said that birth is God's gift.

M: Is it your own experience?

V: (No reply.)

M: It is somebody's momentary enjoyment and I have to suffer for 100 years for it. Is it not? Why should I suffer for somebody's act? Why should I be punished? This is only an example.

From the five elements there is a flow of consciousness in various forms. The five elements do not suffer. Only the forms suffer because of the consciousness. In human form the suffering is more due to the hopes that the future is bright and I must live for that. All this is the play of the primary illusion. When you are sick, you take some medicine. Did your sickness die?

V: I survived, as the sickness vanished.

M: The sickness did not die, but your suffering ended. To summarise all this, since when have we become miserable?

V: Since the appearance of our knowingness.

M: That is it. Now, is this knowingness misery or an ocean of pleasure?

V: (Silence.)

M: The hopes about future are only in the human form. But is there any existence of any tangible entity in the human form, which can prosper in future?

I want to continue my existence but as what? Of what type? Who will give me a reply?
The birth is not of a human form, but of misery in human form. Is it not?

V: (No reply.)

M: The five elements, the *gunas*, the cosmic substance and the cosmic spirit- there is a union of all these ten, at the core of which there is the "I taste". I do not have any knowledge, but when a visitor comes, however scholarly and full of arrogance, I know that he does not know anything.

When one is unconscious, under the influence of chloroform, the operation is done. One feels pain on regaining consciousness. All our worldly activities happen in our semi-conscious state. We feel the pain later on, when we become more sensible.

V: How did you realize yourself?

M: I had full faith in my Guru. I abided in his words. Rest of the happening was spontaneous.

V: Can we know your Guru's words?

M: "You are all that exists. Presently you are the consciousness. God, *Ishwara* etc. are the names of what you are." These words were enough to change me completely.

V: Tell me more about your present existence.

M: I am self-supporting. I do not need any grace or support from outside. It is not that somebody has protected me and I am. I am that which remained unaffected in several dissolutions of the universe.

V: But you look so simple, like us.

M: Those who visit me, will judge me by their own concepts.

V: Why most people do not go to the end of spirituality?

M: They are not in search of Truth, but only peace and happiness. When they get it, they are satisfied and they settle there.

ɞ

November 28, 1979

NOTHING EXISTS;
BUT APPEARS TO EXIST

≥

Maharaj: I am not the body, which is only food essence. I am not the consciousness, which is the quality of the food essence. One has to proceed this way.

Visitor: Then who am I?

M: You are not that which is known; but you are the knower.

V: What is the cause of ignorance?

M: It is because of *Maya*, the illusion. Because of that there is a kind of stupefaction and obscuration of the intellect. The use of words is for a better understanding. In meditation there are no words, but only understanding.

V: What does an advanced seeker find?

M: He knows that he is neither *Maya* nor *Brahman*.

V: Does a *Jnani* suffer to see the death of a tree or of any living being?

M: You suffer because your existence is restricted to a body.

A *Jnani* is infinite and boundless. Hence, there is no pain. In the ocean there are billions of waves. But the ocean is unaffected.

V: My suffering is because I feel oneness with the living form, when it is dying.

M: To overcome that, you must know the Self as unlimited.

V: Can we say that the living beings have no existence?

M: Nothing exists; everything appears to exist. The existence is like sunlight. It vanishes, but does not die. Things appear and disappear. There is no destruction. Hence, a *Jnani* is not troubled by events.

V: So we suffer because of our misunderstanding.

M: Take the case of two neighbouring villages. The people in the two villages might have business and other activities; but does one village know the other village? Does Pune know Mumbai? Does Pune know the town of Ahmednagar, which is next to it? The names *Maya, Brahman, Parabrahman* are like Pune, Mumbai etc. What applies to Mumbai, Pune also applies to *Brahman, Maya* etc. The people of Mumbai may fight with those of Pune; but has Mumbai done anything good or bad to Pune. Just as the cities like Mumbai, Pune do not do anything; but people make a living, *Parabrahman* does not do anything, but everything happens in Its presence.

In Mumbai, there is a temple called Mumbadevi. People have made the idol. When worshipped, the Godess gives what is desired.

Similarly, in every village there are temples constructed by people and the Gods are named after the villages. Mumbadevi means Godess (*devi*) of Mumbai. *Parabrahman* is the complete. It is formless, hence bodiless and has no limbs. It has no expectations from you, it does not need to please you.

V: How can I realize the *Parabrahman* in me?

M: For that you must learn to remain in the bodiless state. With your body identity, there is no chance of realization even after innumerable births. The body identity will remain till the end. Always remember that your existence is independent of your body and I am pointing out the same to you. All depends on your faith.

V: I do have full faith in you.

M: Your present experience of being is like sickness. I did exist without this beingness. All my activities are not to enjoy this sickness, but to make it tolerable. Even deep sleep is a medicine for this illness. My true Self is without this sickness.

V: Hundreds must have benefited from your teachings.

M: I have put in great effort and energy imparting this knowledge to many. But do not ask me what they are doing with it.

V: Please explain.

M: They are busy with their mundane affairs. What else can they do? In order to benefit, one must be fit first. It is not possible to teach everyone from A, B, C.

Our form and identity is changing every moment. From childhood to old age, so many stages came and passed by. This old body is also going to drop. Why worry about that which is changing all the time? When you yourself are changing all the time, what you learn or possess, how will all that remain with you?

❧

November 29, 1979

YOU ARE NOT CONFINED
TO YOUR BODY

Visitor: Should I give up my mundane life for spiritual progress?

Maharaj: Give up your body identity. Always remember that you are not the body. Then do what you like.

V: Should I meditate?

M: Remaining with full awareness that you are not the body is meditation.

You know that you have a body because of your consciousness. In the beginning, knowing that you are not the body, let consciousness be your form.

V: I find it difficult to forget that I am the body.

M: Forget the past. Now you are here and you are told what you are. Have faith and the needful will happen slowly.

V: What is the difference between the *mumukshu*, one who desires to be liberated and a *Sadhaka*, a spiritual seeker?

M: A *mumukshu* has a body; but the seeker is bodiless. Because of your body identity, death and rebirth apply to you.

V: What is the difference between a Seeker and a Sage or *Siddha*?

M: A *Siddha* has achieved the ultimate. There is not the slightest of doubt that he is not the body with name and form. He is no more an individual; neither a man nor a woman.

V: One who has spiritual powers, is he a *Siddha*?

M: No. One who is established in the Self, is a *Siddha*.

V: Does a Sage remember his ignorance prior to His becoming a Sage.

M: Just as the Sun does not know darkness, a Sage does not know ignorance.

V: More than Self-knowledge, I wish to get rid of pain.

M: For that you must get rid of ignorance. Then, there will also be no death and rebirth for you. Self-knowledge is like Sunrise. You see things clearly as they are.

V: My body was born, not I.

M: Your form is consciousness or knowledge and the ignorance of birth cannot touch it. Hence, you do not have experience of birth.

You must have the knowledge of consciousness in order to remove all ignorance. The Self must have knowledge of Itself.

V: What happens at the so called death?

M: The vital breath and mind leave the body. As the consciousness is infinite and all pervading, it has no scope to go anywhere. Before going, it is already there. From conscious it becomes non-conscious there only. It is like cooling of hot water, when the fire is removed.

V: What is *Videhi* or bodiless existence?

M: Because of the *sattva* food body, I come to know that I am. That does not mean that I am the body. I am separate from the body and all pervading. The body has a form and is given a name. But the name and form do not apply to me.

V: Has the *Atma* or Self any "I amness" or I taste.

M: No. There is only pure Being. That is the non-dual state. With body identity, comes the "I" with a separate form. The me and the mine follow. All his experiences, he takes as his knowledge. All these lead to bondage.

V: We hear about revival of the so called dead, on way to cremation. What is the sure sign that a person is dead?

M: It is necessary to wait and watch the skin of the person. If you notice beginning of swelling on the skin, that is a sure sign that the vital breath has left the body. The absence of swelling indicates the presence of vital breath in the body, which can lead to revival.

V: When I see you in front of me, how do you say that you are unborn.

M: If we were born, we must have knowledge of our birth. Do you have knowledge of your birth?

V: No.

M: You have formed a habit of believing whatever you are told. I do not do that. I will not sign the papers seeking my confirmation that I was born.

Is waking state possible without existence of sleep state prior to it?

V: No.

M: Waking is knowledge and sleep is ignorance. The sleep gives strength to the waking state to exist and continue for some time.

One state is always followed by the other.

V: Does it mean that as long as we are in the body, we are asleep?

M: You are not confined to your body; you are everywhere. The limitation is your imagination. Sleep is a must for the knowledge or waking state to follow. Every human form is a child of ignorance. Let us stop here, as now it is time for our evening *bhajans*.

November 30, 1979

SINCE WHEN ARE YOU AND DUE TO WHAT?

Maharaj: You know that you are, that you exist. That memory of yours is the quality of the food essence of your body. If that food juice loses its wetness, your beingness will vanish. The food juice is called *sattva*, whose quality is consciousness or beingness. The word *sattva* is made of *sat* (existence) and *tva* (you). It means you are in reality the existence. In every living form the consciousness is always accompanied by the vital breath. All the activities happen due to the vital breath.

One comes to know that one is, because of the food body. But who comes to know, that cannot be said. All our thinking in this regard is only an imagination or a concept. Mr. or Mrs. Somebody is a concept.

This applies to all of you. You are without name and form. You imagine that you are your body and the name given to it, is your name. If you were not given a name, what would you have said as your name?

Visitor: Nothing.

M: You have accepted your name, as you were repeatedly told to do so. Name is useful for practical purposes like addressing you and in school, college and for bank accounts etc.

V: I find that my anger and hatred are increasing and my capacity to remain aloof from body-mind is becoming weaker.

M: There is no question of anger and hatred when you do not have a body. Your sense of being is not you; it is the quality of the food body. Understand this properly.

V: But I am worried because my mental control is becoming less.

M: True knowledge of yourself is the only solution to your problem. With that knowledge, your hopes, desires and cravings will vanish; with that, anger and hatred will also go. When you see yourself as formless, all your problems will lose their resting place.

V: What is the difference between identifying with the body-mind and not identifying with beingness.

M: There is no difference?

V: May I come to my original question?

M: Is there any question prior to your so-called birth? When a child is born, what is its original question? Our knowledge "we are" (our consciousness) is material knowledge. Is it not?

For the new born, the sense of being was dormant and its development took place during the first three to four years. Without looking at the root to the child consciousness, to the origin of consciousness, people are asking irrelevant questions.

Have you given a thought to the root of consciousness?

V: (No reply.)

M: For some months the child's body is a lump of flesh. What is there other than food material? Since When are you and due to what? Due to what has the root or child appeared? What is the cause of the consciousness?

There is life as long as the body material is moist. If the moisture goes, there will be no life. What we talk here, you may not be able to appreciate.

December 1, 1979

CONSCIOUSNESS, THE PRIMARY ILLUSION

❧

Maharaj: Your existence is like the appearance of light when a matchstick is struck. There is nothing before and nothing after.

With what equipment are you going to begin your search? When the light (consciousness) is extinguished, it is all over-nothing before and nothing after.

Presently, what I am experiencing is material knowledge. Beingness is the quality of the food body. I am talking this from my stand point. Now, I am experiencing my beingness. What control do I have to continue it? I do not need to continue it even for a moment more. With beingness I experience the world. I had enough of it. When I started my search for God, it was enough for me to look into the origin of myself, of my consciousness. There was a time, when I did not exist. Now I exist. What is all this? What is the meaning of my non-existence? – of my non-existence prior to my so-called birth? That is all that I looked into. I was shown my parents etc., which was like viewing a serial on the T.V. I understood its meaning. In short, I investigated the transition from my non-being to being. For me, it was important to find out as to how beingness appeared from my non-being state. If I am asked, how was I 100 years ago, how can I reply? My beingness was absent.

God may be great, but to me that was less important than my appearance from non-being to being.

Yesterday, I told visitors that our experience of the world was full of strife and excessive strife. What have you to say about that? In the past, there were hundreds of wars including the two world wars. Have you ever seen any peace in this world? The strife is not only between countries – it is within every country – within every person. Is it not? I did not struggle for my well-being and prosperity; but only to find the origin of my beingness. Also, my beingness is timebound – ready to vanish any time. Under these circumstances, what can I expect from God, however great he may be?

If I had any control over my beingness, I would have given due importance to God. God may give me prosperity; but what is its use, if I can lose my beingness any moment. When I was not, there were no problems. The sense of being was uncalled for, time bound and depended on food essence.

Our knowingness is seasonal, like rainy season. The season lasts for sixty to one hundred years. All this is my observation. You are free to examine it yourself.

How much will my existence be useful to me? These observations are not meant for the common man. He may lose his hopes, desires and cravings. Life is a struggle, which demands ambition, courage and energy. This knowledge will render a man unfit to struggle. One must have capacity to turn dust into gold. These mundane qualities are a must for experiencing the world. Otherwise, you will live as if the world is not. With the reduction in the hopes and desires, your world will also fade into non-existence.

In order to sustain life, one should be ready to do anything that the time demands. For that, some have to rule their countries, some have to clean toilets and some have to even beg for survival. One has to do all this in order to endure knowingness.

The knowingness also gives hopes for future well-being, which is the motive force for all activities. After all, what one wants is to continue, to be, to exist. There is self-love, the love to be; that must not vanish.

Bhagwan Shri Krishna has explained the gist of Upanishads to Arjuna in *Bhagavad Gita*. This was translated into Marathi by Sage Jnaneshwar. That book is called *Dnyaneshwari*. But his elder brother and Guru Nivrutti Nath commented that it was only a translation and not original work. "Now write something of your own." Then, Jnaneshwar (Dnyaneshwar) wrote a book called *Amrutanubhava*. Having realized the Immortal, Jnaneshwar has put It into words. There is no death at all. Having realized this, he took *Maha Samadhi* (dropped his body), when he was only 21 years old. What is all this? Does anyone think on these lines. What is immortality? Is it to witness the so-called death? Jnaneshwar had no experience of death. The same is here (in my case). When I was not born at all, how can I die? If there was no birth, how did this form appear? That has been shown on the T.V. I call it as a chemical. Our Guru's Guru Sri Bhausaheb Maharaj's photo is there. Who has captured and what is holding the picture? He is wearing only a dhoti; but the picture is so alive. What is holding the picture for a hundred years? I call it a 'Chemical'.

In this world, all the appearances are due to this 'Chemical' and the activities are due to the 'Mechanical'. There is no God, no devotee, no *Maya* and no *Brahman*.

What have you to say about all this? How a living form delivers a living form like itself? – a human from a human being, a lion from a lion, a donkey from a donkey? The chemical energy which has a mind takes these photographs and the energy itself takes the same form. All the skill and growth of the form is due to the "Mechanical".

We think that all development needs training. Now, take the case of a very ill natured poor boy. He rises to the stature of a Sage and people worship him. The ancient kings are easily forgotten; but people remember and worship this Sage. How has all this happened? Has anybody done it or helped it to happen? A temple is constructed in his name, on the top of which there is a golden dome weighing a ton. In Pune, there lived a Sage called Jangli Maharaj meaning a Sage from a jungle.

The so-called-birth is the appearance of the waking state, sleep state and the knowingness. As long as these three states are there, the thirst, hunger and activities for their satiety will go on.

Many incarnations have happened in the past; but who could stop creation, maintenance and destruction? I am not at all proud of my knowledge. What control do I have over anything? Even Brahma, Vishnu and Mahesh (Shiva) could not do anything that lasted long. What I call as 'Chemical Power' is termed the Supreme Consciousness or primary illusion (*Moola Maya*). The behavior or activities are because of *sattva*, *rajas* and *tamas*, which lead to mental modifications. The witnessing of the activities happens due to *sattva* – the news "I Am." All the happening is due to the three qualities and there is no you and I in it. The time limits are decided by *Mahat Tattwa* or the Great Reality. Brahma, Vishnu and Mahesh exist for millions of years. That is long, but not unlimited. That indicates how long the *sattva* quality of the Great Reality lasted for these deities. The total of lives of all the deities – some billions of years – amount to a moment of the primary illusion – it means all was false.

The life spans of Brahma, Vishnu and Mahesh are different from one another. I call them as clocks; i.e. the clock named Brahma, how long did it tick. The clock named Vishnu ticked ten times longer and the Mahesh clock ticked ten times that of Vishnu. The clock named *Moola Maya* ticked only once, to equal to total time of all three. Thereafter, what happened to all of them. Nothing, as it was all an illusion.

I have been talking for the last forty years. There were so many visitors. What are they doing now? They are all busy with their family affairs. That is their first duty, which they have to do. It is in the film and it has to happen that way.

Should I continue expounding spiritual knowledge? When I talk, what is in front of me? Others also talk, but what is in front of them? Whose information are they giving? When somebody talks, it must refer to something.

My beingness, however long, it has to vanish one day. What is the use of all this? The beingness has appeared from the non-being state. If I were aware of it, I would not have allowed my beingness to appear. I would have kept myself aloof from it. But it appeared without my knowledge. I must know the why and how of it.

First, it occurred to me that I should ask God about the appearance of my beingness. But in my non-being state where was God? Many came to me and offered help. But I told them, without your giving anything, whatever I already possess, that's enough for me.

In my case, everything is under my control except my being, which is really a non-being. I have neither birth nor death. I am untouched by any action. What does it mean? Do people think on these lines? Everywhere we see only blind following. With all this background, I am doing *Bhajans*, four times daily.

December 2, 1979

You Were Absent On Your First Birth-Day

࿓

Maharaj: When did one become aware of one's bondage?

Visitor: After one was already in bondage.

M: You will know, when you become That. The guess work is of no use.

We hear everyone talking. Even a child talks. Everything is correct and in order, for the time being. But the sum total of all talk is zero.

I must myself know about me, how my beingness appeared from the non-being state. Many come here and tell about their Gurus. I tell them that I know it. Your Guru is as great as a mountain. He is greater than what you know him. Do not leave him. In reality there is nothing. Everything adds up to nothing. In the past so many things happened. But what is there today? It is as if nothing ever happened. Nothing good or bad has ever happened; nothing will happen to anybody. All this is very clear to me. Then why disturb them?

Somebody, who does not know me, gives my information. How is that possible?

V: (No reply.)

M: You are a judge. Give your judgement. Prior to the appearance of my beingness, I was in the non-being state. Otherwise, I would have stopped it. Why should I lie in a filthy place for nine months for the appearance of this un-called for beingness. i.e. in the mother's womb – What an obnoxious place!

There was no reason for me to accept all that was happening. That chemical was creating my body for nine months. Would you ever have allowed being in that stinking place? You could have stopped it, only if you had prior knowledge of its happening. Such things can happen only in the state of non-being.

Many crores were spent to construct a building. It took ten years to complete it. Today is its inauguration. Similarly, when your beingness began its appearance – what was its starting point?

An astrologer notes the date and time of delivery, for making a prediction. The real birth is the date and time of conception and not the delivery. There is an error of 9 to 10 months in the time noted. How can the predictions come true? But people believe it. They say that the position of the planets is bound to affect the new-born. I had pointed out this error to an elderly astrologer during our visit to Sirpur near Dhule. What is the starting point of your belief that your are. (The word planet means *graha* in Marathi; and the word *graha* also means belief.) It is not the position of the planets that affects your future; but it is your belief in astrology that affects you. You make your consciousness believe and consciousness is God itself. What consciousness believes, it happens. It is the misuse of a great hidden power. You put your stamp of acknowledgment on the astrological predictions and invite trouble for you.

What you do not believe, cannot trouble you. The pregnant Hindu women do not view a lunar eclipse, as they believe in its bad effects. The same is viewed by the Muslim pregnant women, without any ill effects. They do not believe in its bad effects. The Hindu ladies are scared as there are cases of deliveries of deformed babies by viewing an eclipse.

When did the belief that we are, that we exist, began? It is the time since when we remember certain events in our life, like going to school, being beaten by parents or teacher, first time riding a cycle or first time enjoying the birth-day celebrations etc. Prior to that all events were happening, but in the absence of your beingness. This first day is approximately when you were three to five years old.

Prior to the appearance of your beingness, your state was the same as it was ten days prior to your conception. Hence, I say that you were absent on your first, second and perhaps the third birth-day celebrations. It was the food material that was born and not you. Your arrival was three to five years after the birth of the body.

You feel that you are endowed with knowledge and that you have realized *Brahman*. But you are ignoring the main point and that is your true identity. Without taking into account the One who is talking, your talk has no meaning.

When the ignorant talk about Ram and Krishna, they can be excused. They are not told what they are and it is only ignorance that is talking. But when you talk about Ram and Krishna, it must be remembered that it is Ram or Krishna that is talking.

Paramatma or *Parabrahman* is ever present, but Its

existence is like non-existence. In other words It exists in an unknowable state. Hence, if a Sage exists unnoticed, that is in perfect order.

From *Parabrahman* there is existence of the five elements, three *gunas* (qualities), *Prakriti* and *Purusha*. In that the Sun, moon and all the stars are included. When I was in the non-being state all this creation had not happened. All of them appeared with the appearance of my beingness. My non-being is a perfect state – it is the timeless, untainted *Parabrahma* without beingness. It is the Truth and ever existent. In all existence, you cannot point out even a single thing as ever existent.

❧

December 3, 1979

Consciousness
The Formless God
⚜

Maharaj: May God give you long life of over a hundred years. In these years, your identities will go on changing; no identity will stick to you till your end. You will say I was like this, I was like that. Finally, your identity as a very old man will also vanish. If every identity changed from time to time, what is your achievement, which you can say, "This I am?" With what definite identity are you going to continue and enjoy your possessions?

In this whole world can you point out even a single thing which is changeless? With this background, a Sage throws all knowledge overboard. He is free of knowledge.

Without the food body the consciousness cannot appear. In other words, for beingness to appear, a food body form is a must. With passing time, millions of bodies appear. All these bodies are time bound. After their time, they again merge into the five elements. The consciousness appears due to the mutual attraction between the cosmic substance and the cosmic spirit. With consciousness appears the world experience. The mutual love keeps the world alive.

Visitor: How does a Yogi go into *Samadhi*?

M: The Yogi closes the six chakras – *Muladhar, Swadhishthan, Manipur, Anahat, Vishuddha, Adnya* (or *Ajna*) in the spine and resides in the *Sahasrar* centre in the head. Now, please tell me what is that which is responsible for your present form?

V: I have another question. After dying where does one go?

M: On hearing a shocking news, one becomes unconscious. Where did one go? Because one regains consciousness, you do not call it as death. In the so-called death the consciousness does not reappear. Consciousness does not go anywhere. The body becomes unfit for its manifestation.

V: What we hear from others is quite different.

M: In a Sage, the words come from *Nirvikalpa* or direct perception. It is not imagined or learnt knowledge.

V: You rarely comment on other Gurus or Mahatmas.

M: In order to wake you up, I take you to your origin. I talk about child consciousness, in which beingness is initially dormant. Just as a raw mango ripens with time, beingness appears in the child consciousness. I have known the child consciousness and I talk about it. How can I criticize others? When I criticize somebody, what should I take him to be? Should I take him as he appears – an individual soul or as per his true nature? Should I consider his height, weight and colour? I am unable to criticize anybody. Only the ignorance in judgement can lead to criticism.

I want to tell again and again that the body formation happens unknowingly and the knowingness comes after three to five years. He, she or it or anybody is that knowingness. One does not take external help to know one's knowingness.

One has to depend totally upon oneself. A child may become anything- poor or rich, ignorant or a Sage; but what was at the root, which enabled everything to happen? What is the seed or root of any happening? The root or seed is the same for all. It originates from food juices out of five elemental vegetation. Our consciousness resides in the consumed and digested food juices.

In the food originates the movement due to the vital breath, accompanied by consciousness or the sense of being. The language of the vital breath is the mind. Only the food body has a form; but it cannot be anybody's identity. All the rest i.e. vital breath, mind and the consciousness are formless. There is no white, black, short or tall there. The consciousness is also referred to as *Mahat Tatwa*, *Brahmasutra* or *Hiranyagarbha*. Without our sense of being how can we recognize God, or *Ishwara*? When I have known my own origin, is it necessary for me to search for other's origin? I never go to meet any Gurus, Saints or Sages. If anybody invites me to meet any Mahatma, I tell him that his Guru is really great like a mountain.

What I am at source, others are the same. For every living being there is the food body and the sense of being along with the vital breath. The birth of every living being is the appearance of waking state, sleep and the sense of being. Those who cannot understand or accept this simple truth about their origin, go from place to place in search of knowledge. They imagine and write their own destiny; and they suffer accordingly.

You get bound or hanged by your own concepts. One who does not know one's own origin, how can he be expected to know other's origin? But people become Gurus and anybody can have a following. All knowledge, however great, is all useless, if it does not include the knowledge of one's own source.

If the greatness of a Guru is to be judged by counting the number of his followers, one's vast knowledge can also similarly make one great.

Always remember that the greatest thing is your consciousness, without which you cannot even notice the great world. If your knowingness is not, what can you know? Without your knowingness, is there any pain or pleasure for you?

A child may say anything; but for its age all that is in perfect order. While assessing, one has to consider the times and the age. After knowing his bodiless nature, what a Sage talks, that is also in order. You must note here that now he knows that he is not the body. Hence, his utterance is the Truth.

In the history, you read many different utterances. You must take a note of the times when they were said. It was correct for that time. The effect of the time is such that statements are made without thought of the consequent trouble and suffering. The time provides the motive force for the events to happen. Now, while sitting on the floor, I have to take help of my hands in order to get up. This is the result of the time that has passed. The changes happen as per the passing phase. A young man could fight with an elephant. That was also a passing phase. Later he could not do it. Where are these phases decided? At the so-called-birth, in the astral body, the necessary changes happen.

All the future happenings are not determined by the world, but in the astral body. All the future happenings are filmed and are ready to unfold as per the passing phases.

At my eighty three years age, I have to hold a tea cup with both the hands. What is wrong with me? Sufficient aging has taken place in the child which appeared eighty three years ago.

I call it Har Har Mahadeo, i.e. it is all getting over. What is a doctor's job? It is to try to hold the consciousness in the body of the patient – not to allow it to vanish. For any reason, if the nourishment does not reach the consciousness, it cannot remain in the body. Because consciousness is the quality of the food essence, proper food supply is a must.

In order to see, you need light. This light is provided by burning food in your body, i.e. in your stomach. Consciousness is luminous and Godly and it is called *Bhagwan* or *Vasudeo*. The consumed food sustains your beingness. The Supreme Consciousness or the great Reality resides in your food material. Food is necessary to keep your memory "I Am" intact.

There was time, when I existed as if not; and there was no struggle to survive. From that state the present time bound state has appeared, which needs sustenance. I know the secret of transition from the trouble free state to the troublesome.

There was a time when my beingness was not present. I came to know the appearance of the beingness. I am it's witness. This transition from the non-knowing state to the present knowing state, itself is a miracle. How this transition took place, that is all that I saw. This transition applies to every living form. But a rare one in the human form knows the secret of how it happens.

December 4, 1979

KNOW YOUR ETERNAL STATE

Maharaj: Our existence is there until the food material, because of which the child consciousness appeared, sustains beingness. When the material gets dried up, our consciousness vanishes. Have you read "I am That"?

Visitor: Yes.

M: After Self-knowledge, it is difficult to sustain beingness. The vital breath suddenly leaves the body. In case of Shri Krishna, He continued despite knowing Self fully.

V: It is said that Bhagwan Krishna attained the highest state of realization.

M: He is perfect in all respects. He could easily mix with the small or the big. He had no pose or stance of any kind. He was in the most natural state called the '*Sahaja-Awastha*'.

V: It is said that life is a circle; one goes where one began.

M: An infant has no memory; it cannot recognize anybody. A very old man loses all knowledge and memory. He is almost like an infant. The old man is alive as long as the child principle exists. When that is no more, the man is declared dead by the people around him. But a Sage calls it liberation and not death.

V: You always give stress on our consciousness, why?

M: You may have all the knowledge contained in an encyclopedia; but what is your first knowledge?

V: First I know that "I Am". That is my first knowledge.

M: If that first knowledge is absent, what is the use of all your rest of the knowledge, however great?

V: It is all useless.

M: That is the importance of the knowledge "you are" or of your consciousness. If that vanishes, what can you enjoy? You may be a very rich man. Without consciousness what is the use of all your wealth? Then, what is great: wealth or consciousness?

V: Is it enough, if we keep in mind what we hear from you?

M: No. It should not remain at the verbal level. Take the example of how the cattle get their nourishment from grass. They eat it, chew it and then ruminate. You must assimilate what you hear, the same way. You must make it your own. Then, there will be no need to remember it.

V: What is the difference between a disciple and his Guru?

M: The first is *Atma* and the second *Paramatma*. The first has knowledge and the second transcends knowledge. Crores of Dynamic *Brahman*s play in the Sadguru.

V: When I wake up from deep sleep, first I know "I Am" and I notice the world.

M: Your world is in your consciousness, as sunlight is in the Sun.

When there is consciousness, there are the five elements, three *gunas*, *Prakriti* and *Purusha*.

V: If I am so great to have this great consciousness, the Self-realization should become easy for me.

M: How can Self-realization be a result of concepts?

V: It is said that God is great.

M: God and the primary illusion may be great; but without your beingness, who will recognise their greatness. You must always be conscious of the greatness of your consciousness. You are never your body. That is also very important.

V: Truth or the Absolute must be full of knowledge.

M: On the other hand, It does not have even the slightest touch of knowledge. This is not a hearsay, but my own eternal experience. The use of the word 'experience' is only for your understanding. In Reality that word has no place.

This bodily experience is a nuisance for me. It is like picking up an infant left on the road and then taking trouble to bring it up. Just as one who lifts the infant was not concerned with it, I am not concerned with the world and its experience. There was no compulsion to take care of the child, but it happened out of pity. Could you have avoided it?

V: No.

M: The Yogis and ascetics are in search of Truth. Only the Eternal can be called as the Truth. Is it not?

V: Yes.

M: The association of Truth is very normal for me. My present beingness is like a painful pimple. Since time immemorial, I am acquainted with the Eternal and the Truth – whatever they are. None can be a witness to this.

V: What is your reaction to envy, hate and quarrel in the world?

M: I dislike people troubling others and inflicting pain on them. But people cannot give up their wrong tendencies.

I ask my beingness, "you were not there and you are bound

to vanish after a short period. What do you want? What will satisfy you? Why are you struggling so much?" What is the use of the sense objects, when your beingness will be no more?

V: That is also our experience about our beingness.

M: Whatever you see and do, you instantly know that, it was not there prior to the so-called birth.

Everybody has directly or indirectly taken initiation as per the religion to which he or she belongs. Is it not important to know that principle, which takes the initiation? Is it not necessary to find out what is the nature of that principle? Who will give me replies to my questions?

V: Many such questions haunt us without any lasting solution.

M: All living beings are struggling all the time. As compared to the Eternal, all existence is momentary. It is only an appearance, without any substance. Human existence is like the day-dreaming of an idle person lying in bed. All human wants are the desires of a non-entity. As compared to the Eternal, the momentary existence of any form is really a non-existence. Then why take all the trouble?

Suppose, at present, I want to exist, I want to be. But how should I be, how should I look like, what should be my nature and in what form should I exist? All human thinking is guided by emotions and tradition. The same is also the origin and the content of every human form.

V: Recently, I have started reading a book called *Amrutanubhav* written by the Sage Jnaneshwar, with commentary by Mr. P.Y. Deshpande.

M: I will tell Mr. Deshpande, you are great to have done this work. Who comes first, the experience or the experiencer?

V: Of course, the experiencer comes first.

M: What is the nature of the experiencer? And what is his experience of immortality? What is your observation?

V: I cannot comment; so far I have read only a few pages.

M: Who is it that behaves? The three *gunas* or qualities: *Sattva*, *Rajas* and *Tamas* do all the activities. Who makes use of the qualities in order to behave? *Sattva* is the quality of the five elements of which the first is space. The interaction or the conflict between the elements ultimately lands on the surface of the earth. Then, vegetation is created with various forms. From that are created the other living beings. Out of these, the best is the human form.

What is Eternal, is the only Truth. There is no coming and going or appearance and disappearance for it. As Reality is one and only one, there cannot be any witness to it. What is going on is the ephemeral called the world. As compared to the Eternal, the worldly existence is momentary – as if not.

All the experiences of a life span, are restricted to that span only. There is no continuity of experiences from one life to another.

The Eternal does not have the slightest touch of the primary illusion. The sense of being or the consciousness is absent in the Eternal. One who feels that one is blessed, cannot be realized. As long as there is the idea of virtue or of religious merit, there are no hopes of Self-realization.

Your present state is untrue, as it is changing and not Eternal. You have to know your Eternal state.

Whatever I was not, I threw away all that, overboard. After disposing off all my so called being, I have also disposed of my non-being as well. I am the Eternal, which cannot be described as this or that.

My observation is in line with the following verse of Swami

Ramdas in his book *Dasbodh*: "Whatever appeared, all that disappeared, whatever was not, it did not exist. Whatever was left over from the above two, that remained, but beyond all description."

In this whole world, one who cannot find a witness to One's true being, is a rare One. A devotee of God is protected by God and He is devotee's witness; but a Sage cannot find a witness to his true being. There is no witness other than the Sage himself.

If a visitor insists on his own stand, I encourage him to hold on to it. My only condition is that he should be fully satisfied with his own stand. There should be no disturbance from his mind.

All our problems and our efforts to find a solution are due to the appearance of the beingness. In deep sleep and also after Self-realization, when the beingness disappears, the problems are over.

When you are ignorant; you can minimise your difficulties by avoiding hurting others.

That *Ishwara* died in one; then what happened ? – the same as it has happened here (Maharaj points to himself).

My words are difficult to understand and still more difficult to accept.

❧

December 5, 1979

YOUR CONSCIOUSNESS
IS A CHEAT

Maharaj: In this world we observe peoples' grief as a matter of convenience.

Visitor: How is that ?

M: A husband is in pain to see his wife dead. If we watch a woman when her husband dies, it appears that she may soon join her husband. But we are shocked to hear about her remarriage.

V: What is the reason?

M: You do not know what you are. What you think yourself to be goes on changing without your permission and knowledge. Then, how can your feelings and promises remain unchanged?

V: That is true.

M: Consider your own case, your own past. You will be surprised to see what you were and what were your thoughts, as compared to your present condition. Your own identity is changing from time to time: from a dashing young man to a bedridden old man, who is to be fed by a spoon in his last days.

Is there any honesty, any consistency in what you think you are? What is your identity, which is under your control?

V: I am interested in Yoga.

M: What is Yoga? It is your union with your ideal. When you try to get anything, you have to consider what will be your identity, when you get it. If it is going to take a long time for getting something, you are not likely to be the same as you are now.

Due to the uncertainty involved in it, the striving for something becomes meaningless.

If you go into the outer space and due to certain technical problems you cannot return to earth, your food supply is bound to finish. Then what will happen to your beingness? Your confidence that you are, what will happen to it?

Does your self confidence depend upon the world or upon the food juices that are consumed? If your existence is so much dependable, what is the use of struggling to do this and that? The proof of your being, is in the food material. Our beingness is so much dependent as if it is meaningless.

If somebody has a vision of *Ishwara*, there is no need to feel great about it. That vision does not make him independent of food material. When the food juices get dried up, the beingness leaves even without making an announcement.

The various words in the Sanskrit language appear to be originated under the influence of the knowers of Truth. Take the word *Satwa* or *Sattva*, which is the first guna or quality. The quintessence of food is called *Sattva*. This word is split into *Sat + tva*. *Sat* means existence and *tva* means you. Hence, *Sattva* means the existence which is 'you'. The quality of the food essence is the knowledge 'you are'. It is the Eternal you, which comes to know that It exists. Without a food body the Eternal does not know that It exists.

This is not mere knowledge for you, but it is your own experience. Because of your body you, the Eternal, know that you are. When your body was not, you did not know about it.

The Eternal does not need food to sustain Itself. But the consciousness, which is the expression of the Eternal, needs food essence – *Sattva* – to sustain itself. One, who knows the source of consciousness, realizes the Eternal and realises the Eternal as his/her Eternal State.

V: When the beingness leaves the body, can we call it death?

M: Death is the wrong word. We can call it liberation. When hot water cools, we do not call it death. The cooling of body, when beingness is no more, is similar. People say that I am a *Dnyani* (commonly written as *Jnani*). What do I know? I only know that the knowledge 'you are' or your consciousness is a perfect cheat. You love your beingness, although it is intolerable. This paradox is the cheating. Even a bed-ridden person, breathing his last, wants more life. He has lost everything, including memory. His close relatives have to get themselves introduced to him again and again.

You might have earned great religious merit, but what will be your ultimate form to take it all along with you. When the drop merges with the ocean, where can it keep its earnings and certificates. What is the relation between the knowledge "you are" and the knowledge collected by you during your lifetime? When the knowledge "you are" itself becomes no-knowledge, where is the accumulated knowledge? What control do you have over anything, when your very being is out of your control. When our beingness vanishes, as if, it never existed, what is left behind to talk about?

The world is full of paradoxes.

M: The word *Ananda* or the bliss is very liberally used as in *Sadananda*, This *ananda* and That *ananda*. But remember, *Ananda* is a quality which has no place in the Absolute, which is *Nirguna* or non-qualitative. The bliss has a place as long as there is consciousness, but not beyond.

Most of the people worship God for material gains. They do not need Self-knowledge; and God gives them what they want i.e. worldly possessions and well-being. It is very rare to find a customer for Self-knowledge.

As long as there is consciousness, we can think of sin and religious merit. The consciousness is time-bound. When the consciousness is not, who is there to suffer due to sin or enjoy due to religious merit.

When you know 'you are', with that knowledge you go on accumulating worldly knowledge. When you do not know 'you are', who is there to accumulate?

You think you are like this or like that; but can you assure yourself that you will always be there to think that way?

All our actions and experiences are time-bound. Nothing gives us lasting company, including this talk that is going on now.

V: We cannot take anything with us.

M: Nothing remains with us permanently. Talking about joy or bliss, that is a quality and no quality can remain permanently with us. As long as we know 'we are', these qualities remain.

These talks are like a brush to clean and clear ignorance, so that the Absolute opens up. Mostly people worship God, seeking reward for it. They have no interest in Self-knowledge. People sing devotional songs (*bhajans*) or do meditation in order to get what they want. The true seeker dislikes such devotion and he is a rare one. Our sense of being is Godly. The ultimate purpose of spirituality is to know the Self and be really peaceful. Many a times seekers acquire spiritual powers and they get entangled in it. They think they have achieved the ultimate and that is the end of their spirituality.

V: Instead of meditating on an external object, meditating on the Self within, is this also a kind of worship?

M: That is the normal tradition of approaching the Self. It is their faith, which prompts them to do that.

For all seekers the ultimate destination is the same; but some practices are difficult like pushing a cart, instead of pulling it.

We do not advocate any practices. One who reads *Bhagavad Gita* correctly, reads one's own information in it and not that of Krishna. One sees oneself as immortal, the Eternal. One who takes oneself as the body, remains a *mumukshu* and does not qualify to become a seeker.

M: *Atma* is not just a word, but it is what one is in reality. One loses one's individuality and remains as the Self.

Our sense of being itself is the dynamic *Brahman* or *Maya*. Your existence without the sense of being is *Parabrahman* or the Absolute. When we know 'we are', the world accompanies it with all the problems. Not knowing 'you are', gives you rest and peace. Your attention is incomplete. That which is beyond attention is full and complete.

V: One must act without any expectations.

M: The world is full of activity. The dynamic consciousness (*Chaitanya*) is full of struggle and conflict. When the 'I Am' is gone, all the trouble ends.

V: What is the ultimate in spirituality?

M: All the so called knowledge (*jnana*) turned out to be *Vijnana* or beyond knowledge. The knowledge turned out to be no-knowledge. *Parabrahman* is said to be desireless. It means the Absolute is of no use to Itself. It may be useful to others.

December 6, 1979

MAYA IS SELF-LOVE
❧

Maharaj: With the appearance of 'I love', the space appears with the beginning of the world.

Visitor: With that there is also the appearance of the body and one tends to acquire things for pleasure.

M: This is the initial stage of the dull and the stupid.

V: One develops love.

M: Every living being is born love or love affected. Despite unbearable suffering, there is love to exist. One who knows what this 'I love' is, is liberated, and his 'I love' vanishes.

V: How is *Maya* related to love?

M: Maya is self-love. When we do not know 'we are', that state is in perfect order. When we know 'we are' that is not a problem of an individual, but it is a worldly predicament.

V: Due to this, some renounce all sensuous delight or gratification.

M: We do not find it in the life of Sri Krishna. A sage is unattached and hence unaffected by the worldly attractions and problems.

V: Others are attracted to the objects of the world.

M: One's body identity and ego is responsible for it. The ignorant is conscious of the body, but pure *Brahman* is unconscious of it. Even an infant does not know that it has a body.

V: What is it that leads to peace and tranquility?

M: I am not well. Let us stop here.

December 7, 1979

FIND OUT THE SOURCE
OF 'I AM'
⁊⹀

Visitor: What is the cause of ignorance?

Maharaj: The knowledge 'you are' is the only reliable knowledge. But man has the habit of collecting knowledge from every source and carry the load on his head. He is told about birth and rebirth. Although birth is not his own experience, he takes it as true. Man's knowledge is full of concepts and imagination.

V: What about the law of *karma*? i.e. what we do in this life, the effects we have to suffer in next life.

M: As you take yourself as your body, the law of *karma* affects you. You even try to benefit by it. If you know yourself as the Self, the law will not affect you.

V: The law of *karma* scares us.

M: Our sense of being is the quality of the quintessence of food and the shape of the food material is taken by us as our form. Your Eternal nature is without the sense of being.

When the vital breath leaves the body, it becomes inert. It is like the extinguishing of a flame. Does the flame go anywhere? When the body drops, there is no going anywhere. At the so called birth, there is no coming from anywhere. The Self is everywhere. It does not leave any space to travel to.

M: When I talk, I do not talk about any individual. I talk about the nature of consciousness. The cycle of creation, sustenance and dissolution goes on undisturbed. No Mahatma or incarnation like Ram or Krishna can stop the cycle. I talk about incarnation. What was there prior to calling one an incarnate? What lead to the change from an ordinary person to an incarnate? You never think as to what you were prior to the appearance of the body and how the knowledge 'I Am' which did not exist, began to appear.

You are so much habituated living in concepts that you entertain yourself watching dramas and movies. You get lost in somebody's imagination, devoid of any content. That is how you pass your valuable time.

The fond concepts of a Prophet become a religion for his followers. Instead of following somebody, find out how the confidence 'I Am', which depends upon breathing, made an appearance. Without going to the source of 'I Am', to talk of *Ishwara* and *Brahman*, has no value. Everyone knows that 'I Am' was absent and it suddenly made an appearance. Now, you know 'you are'. Other than this, what is your knowledge? Your main job is to find out the source of 'I Am'.

Take the example of the dream world. When the sense of being appears in deep sleep, the dream world begins with a new body for you.

M: Is not this dream world nothing other than the creation of your consciousness?

V: Yes.

M: While watching a dream one forgets that one is out of the dream and sleeping comfortably in a bed. In reality, witnessing of the dream happens without any involvement. In the dream also there is identification with the dream body, which suffers. The dream world appears to be real until one wakes up. Sometimes one sees oneself dead in dream.

The world takes birth in your consciousness.

The waking state consciousness gives rise to this waking world and the dream consciousness to the dream world.

Nothing exists in the absence of your consciousness. It means our consciousness contains everything.

December 8, 1979

BIRTH AND DEATH IS A MYTH

Maharaj: Our sense of being is the quality of food essence made of the five elements. There is only a food body but no individual. There is manifestation, which contains everything. When there is no individual, who is born and who dies? There is only an appearance and disappearance, like a flame. Coming and going is a myth. The food material or *Sattva* gives strength to the *gunas* or qualities of *Sattva*, *Rajas* and *Tamas*, due to which activities happen. Due to ageing, the food body cannot give sufficient strength for the activity. There is all-round weakness including that of the physique and intellect. When I am not the five elements, I cannot be the body. Hence the three qualities of *Sattva*, *Rajas* and *Tamas* are not mine.

In the three qualities, the main is *Sattva*. Our sense of being is its quality. The *Sattva* provides light and strength to *Rajas* and *Tamas*.

When anything burns there is light. The food body burns giving rise to the light of consciousness, in which you see the world.

Visitor: What is *Atma*?

M: It is not just a word. *Atma* means undivided you. *Atma* or our being cannot be felt without *Sattva* or a food essence body.

December 9, 1979

YOUR EXISTENCE IS A BORROWED BEING

Maharaj: The knower of mind is unaffected by it. One gets involved with the mind due to one's body identity due to one's identification with the body.

Visitor: Normally, our mind controls us.

M: Take the example of a burning incense stick. I get its smell. I am neither the stick nor its smell. Similarly, I smell my presence due to the food body. I am neither the body nor the sense of presence (consciousness).

V: Why did Adi Shankara take *Maha Samadhi* (dropped his body) at an early age?

M: I have nothing to do with the continuation or the exit of this sense of presence.

Breathing is happening continuously. The breath comes in and goes out of the body, inspite of you. If you are not the breath or vital breath how can you be the mind? Because you can see your mind, you are separate from it.

The body is made up of the five elements. When you are not the elements, how can you be the body? Due to ignorance you consider death of the body as your death; but you are that which separates and leaves the body. You have no death.

I have no expectation from this body and its existence, I have no expectation from you. Whether you visit me or not, it does not matter.

Your existence is a borrowed being and time-bound. It is bound to go. What can you expect from it?

V: Why did Shankara depart at a young age?

M: You will know it, when you will be like Him.

V: The other day anger came to me. I do not say that I got angry. With this attitude of separation from anger, can there be irresponsible behaviour?

M: The anger is related to mind. Are you the mind? What are you? Who watches the flow of thoughts?

M: There is no question of identifying with the mind. Even if you identify with consciousness, that also is going to vanish.

V: But we need this consciousness.

M: Without any need of consciousness, you have to suffer because of your consciousness.

V: All our needs are because of the consciousness. Without it there are no needs.

M: You are uttering the words that you have heard. Words cannot describe the liberated.

V: Then what should I do?

M: Do not do that which you feel like doing. But nothing stops, even if there is no need to do it. Your waking in the morning, from what did it arise?

V: (No reply).

V: If one is sure of having Self-knowledge, what do you say?

M: That is a certain sign of being in ignorance. Many visit me seeking my confirmation for their Self-realization; but they fail to get it.

There are many places where Self-knowledge is imparted; but the way it is done here, you may not come across elsewhere.

One has to observe the changeless amongst the changeful. The experience of day and night is changeful, not changeless. The contentment which is dependent, is not true. The true contentment is tasteless, i.e. in the true contentment there is no sense of being. Whatever can be witnessed, cannot be your true Self.

V: If I am fully contented with what I have understood?

M: Then be there only. That is enough.

I do not want to displease anybody; for I am here to uproot the very cause of displeasure.

If somebody becomes happy by coming here, do I need his blessings? If somebody leaves with displeasure, should I seek his pardon? It is not the Self, which becomes happy or unhappy. It is the mind only, which is not important.

V: Although the experiences change, the witness remains the same.

M: That changes, due to which the witnessing happens. You are able to see a distant star using a telescope. Similarly, consciousness is a telescope by which you observe objects. Is it your work?

V: It is the work of consciousness.

M: Witnessing happens. It cannot be called as work. Hence, a witness is not a doer.

V: Our body is also like a telescope.

M: The body is like mud.

V: It is only food material.

M: Whoever may visit me. My talk is not to please anybody. One may see me talking contrary to one's expectations. The listener is hearing with his body identity, as a man or a woman. Hence, the misunderstanding. How can I talk in support of one's ignorance?

I will tell the Truth, whether it agrees with your opinion or not.

In a dream one sees oneself as a five years old boy. He grows to the age of a hundred. He experiences good and bad things and finally dies. The dream ends there due to waking. In the dream, what was true and what was false? In the dream one saw even God Brahma. While watching the dream, the witness of the dream was forgotten and one became a participant in the dream world. To whom did the dream world, including the dream body appear? Is the witness a part of the dream world? Was the dream world seen by the sleeping body or by the dream body? When the dream ended what happened to the God Brahma, seen in the dream? Will He reincarnate?

V: He never existed.

M: In the dream experience, what was false? In deep sleep that sense of waking was false and foolish.

V: If this life is equally false, why did I take this birth?

M: You are telling a lie. Knowingly, you would have never taken birth. It has happened without your knowledge. You came to know about it three to five years later. Knowingly, who would enter the womb to rot for nine months?

❧

December 10, 1979

INTELLECT IS THE PRODUCT OF MIND

Maharaj: In this world you come across different types of forms. All these are time-bound.

Visitor: Do all these forms have the knowledge 'I Am so and so"?

M: That is only in human beings.

V: Does an infant know that it is an infant?

M: It takes three to five years to know it. How old were you when you first recognised your mother?

V: About four years old.

M: Before that you did not even know that you existed.

V: Can we say that the consciousness was dormant?

M: Yes. Like in sleep. The towel can be set on fire. Your consciousness was like fire in this towel. Is there fire in this towel?

V: Yes, dormant. Children utter words. Is it knowledge?

M: That is like a parrot. They do not know what they talk.

Before the age of three, there is no intelligence even to know one's existence. When the knowledge 'I Am' is absent, there cannot be any expectations 'to be'.

V: With Self-knowledge, does it become clear that one is not the consciousness?

M: Who has Self-knowledge? Is it the body?

V: There is nothing that knows.

M: Then who is speaking?

V: I do not know.

M: Then take all this as false.

V: I want more clarification on this.

M: The intellect develops after collection of knowledge. The education is meant to develop intellect. Without proper education and training can you call somebody intelligent?

V: No.

M: Can you teach a two year old child, which does not know 'it is'?

V: No. What is the use of the mind?

M: One has to use one's mind in order to develop the intellect. Intellect is the product of mind.

V: Is not a spiritual mind a handicap in worldly activities?

M: One has to develop a mind to succeed in this world. You feel like asking something profound, but are unable to ask.

V: When I put a question to you, you point out my mistake. That mistake is because of my body identity. Does it mean that all this discussion here is to know that there is nothing?

M: All this is a material talk, a result of food essence.

M: The ultimate purpose is to attain the desireless *Parabrahman* state. At other places, you will be drawn into more and more activities for better achievements.

V: The confidence that we are is useful to us.

M: Without that how will you do your activities?

V: Why do other spiritual teachers refrain from telling the Truth?

M: They have their own interest in it. The promotion of desirelessness will affect their own spiritual business. That must go on. Listening to my talks, one develops the conviction that one's birth itself is a fiction. It has no reality. Obviously, one knows that there is no birth, no death. There is no coming and going. That gives rest to all unnecessary activities.

V: To know intellectually that one is unborn and to realize it actually, these two are not the same.

M: You already know that you are prior to intellect. You are prior to even the consciousness. A hundred years ago you were present, but there was no consciousness. Do you disagree?

V: No.

M: The Eternal knows that there was no consciousness. All that is known through consciousness, is the ephemeral. The so called birth and death, are a part of the transient.

V: What is birth?

M: The appearance of 'I Am' or the sense of being is the so called birth. The Eternal does not have the sense of being. Birth means becoming conscious of one's presence. It took nine months in the womb and a few years outside for the appearance of the sense of being. It is like cooking of food material by heating and stirring and adding salt, chillies etc., for a taste. It took approximately four to six years for the taste 'I Am' to appear. It is not the birth of somebody – he, she or it. The content of the womb was the knowledge 'I Am' in dormant condition.

❧

December 11, 1979

ULTIMATELY, KNOWLEDGE IS IGNORANCE

Maharaj: The so called birth is the appearance of ignorance which prevails till the so called death. A rare one knows this ignorance and observes all the so called knowledge as useless. A *Jnani* finds that the existence is not worth the trouble it demands.

What you learn here, you cannot expect to hear elsewhere. There you will get entangled in activities.

Visitor: What about the purity of *Brahmins* and the untouchability of the lower castes?

M: All these are happenings in sheer ignorance. In Self-knowledge there is no place for knowledge, even that of knowledge 'I Am'. All of it gets washed out. Have you heard this anywhere?

V: No.

M: For some spiritual teachers consciousness is the upper limit. "You are not the body but the dynamic consciousness (*Chaitanya*)". They do not go beyond consciousness.

Even my Guru told me, "You are consciousness God. What is beyond that, you have to find It yourself."

V: Is a Sage always in bliss?

M: This body is on fire. Self-knowledge has a strange quality. Sometimes it is unbearable.

Tanslator: Is it the consciousness that becomes unbearable?

M: How did you ask that question? Other than consciousness what is there to become bearable or unbearable?

In spirituality one attains a state of non-duality. There is neither 'I Am' nor others. When there is one, others are bound to accompany. Self knowledge is profound and mysterious.

When there is one, one needs many. One is never satisfied with the bear minimum necessities. One never tries to experience the bliss of being. Instead, one desires more happiness by ever increasing acquisitions. Why do people struggle for more?

Translator : One cannot be at peace with consciousness and tries to forget it in activity.

M: Are people contented with the bliss of the Self (*Atmananda*)?

M: Does consciousness become conscious of attention or the attention gives attention to consciousness? What is your experience?

You come to know anything because of consciousness. Without your consciousness is there any knowing? Is not knowing painful like a pin-prick? In order to forget it or to make the pain bearable one gets involved in activities.

Without Guru's grace one cannot be out of this trouble.

We take ourselves to be that which, in reality, we are not. That is the cause of all our suffering and unhappiness. If you are everything, there is no fear. The presence of others, is the cause of fear. Is there anybody thinking on these line?

V: No. I have not heard this anywhere.

M: All words come from a source, other than the Self. The Self has no language of Its own. A two year old child has no language of its own. It learns from the mother. Initially, we are free of a language. We learn it from others. What is not ours has to go finally. If we live long, the language leaves us.

V: Is the Self full of happiness?

M: The Self is free of grief, hence it does not need happiness. The Eternal is the only Truth. The untruth is time-bound. It comes and goes. The ignorant have no choice but to live life as it unfolds.

M: The consciousness is Godly, still it cannot give indefinite company to the Eternal. The consciousness cannot be Eternal. A *Jnani* is an expression of the Eternal in a form. He is not the form, but only appears to be so. He is the Eternal.

The consciousness cannot give company to the *Jnani* indefinitely. What does it mean?

Translator: It means consciousness is bound to leave the *Jnani*.

M: Is not living in a form painful? Life is full of trouble. The experience of the Universal Consciousness is full of trouble. Except that, there is no question of profit or loss there. The pain is due to the wrong identity due to ignorance. One is punished for considering oneself as that which one is not. Under these circumstances, should I impart knowledge?

Translator: The earnest seekers need it.

M: There are some people who always go in for the best, including Self knowledge; but they are not prepared to pay the price for It. They save even a beedi without offering it to anybody. People come to listen and depart in the middle of talks, without taking leave.

Some people ask irrelevant questions. I tell them not to waste their time and energy. Only try to find out why and how the beingness made its appearance.

This beingness was absent a hundred years ago. This is your direct knowledge. Why and how it appeared, should also be known directly, without referring to books or to other people.

V: Our knowledge is full of concepts.

M: The concepts sustain ignorance and give rise to fear.

Once there was a Guru sitting amidst his disciples. Every disciple was earlier told separately about a basket, full of garlands. The disciples had to garland the Guru, one by one. In case of any doubt, one could skip the garlanding without telling anybody.

The first disciple lifted the lid of basket and picked a garland. He dropped it immediately in the basket, as it was a cobra. The same was repeated by other disciples. The last disciple who had full faith in his Guru, picked the garland made from fresh cute flowers. This disciple was free of concepts, hence fearless. Concepts lead to delusion and misapprehension.

Consider your beingness as God and worship it with your sense of being only. Thereby, your beingness will become God in reality. God is consciousness or knowledge, Guru is also knowledge. This worship is advocated in the devotion with attributes (*Saguna Bhakti*). This way when one knows this knowledge, its true nature as ignorance becomes clear. Outwardly, what appears as knowledge is pure ignorance at source.

M: This way the knowledge takes away the ignorance and what remains is in perfect order.

V: Then, how should a man behave in the world?

M: If you wish to study a tree, should you watch the foliage or the roots?

V: Roots.

M: Your question does not originate from the roots. If somebody talks something irrelevant, I wring him there only.

V: Why is 'I Am' knowledge so important?

M: Without it did you have knowledge of your world? Then, how can you underestimate it?

V: How to get rid of the birth and death concepts?

M: When you know the origin and cause of your consciousness, there will be no birth or death for you. It is like catching the thief. The 'I Am' knowledge was absent. It has suddenly entered like a thief. Here, the night signifies ignorance. The Eternal never said 'I Am'. This thief which entered is saying 'I Am'. We must find out as to wherefrom this thief entered. This thief did not enter alone but with Cosmic Spirit (*Purusha*) and Cosmic Substance (*Prakriti*) i.e. the male and the female aspect. And what is the meaning of this happening? It is 'I Am', that is all. You were in the state of non-duality, in which the sense of being was absent. Due to this thief the duality started with 'I Am' and the experience of the world.

M: The Cosmic Spirit is the experience of silence, in which there are no words. The words begin with the Cosmic Substance, which is the female aspect. The absence of sense of being is the ideal. The activities begin with the appearance of sense of being. In deep sleep, as well as, in *Samadhi*, the sense of being is absent and there is contentment. The appearance of sense of being is the beginning of conflict. In its absence, there is peace and tranquility.

Elsewhere, you will be taught faithful observance of the

duties for success and happiness. Here I show you the futility of action and remove the very cause of disturbances. I show you, why and how actions are not needed for real contentment.

By activities you may do better for some time; but none of those actions would give you eternal contentment.

In the absence of sense of being there were no needs, including the craving to be or to exist. The sense of being gives rise to all kinds of needs.

The people turn to spirituality only when there is a rise of Self-knowledge in them in dormant condition. Just as the so called birth happens unknowingly, the rise of Self-knowledge happens unknowingly.

In the absence of the knowledge (Sun) rise, people do not develop interest in spirituality. The dormant condition is like the existence of fire in this towel.

Other teachers will tell you how to achieve perfection. None will tell you that you are already perfect prior to doing anything. The question is only of knowing it directly.

M: *(to a new visitor)* : You say you have no Guru. From your talk, it appears, you had a Guru.

V: Really, I have no Guru.

M: You are hiding something. In spirituality you should be frank and open. What do you understand by the term Guru?

V: He is a spiritual teacher.

M: Guru means consciousness or knowledge. When you met him, he woke up the knowledge within you. That is why you have developed interest in Self-knowledge. Spirituality is the give and take of knowledge. Guru, the giver, is knowledge and disciple, the receiver, is also knowledge (*jnana*).

December 12, 1979

CAN READING SCRIPTURES HELP?

ッ

Maharaj: Due to ignorance, people identify with their bodies. This identity has an end by getting burnt or getting buried. What you are in reality, as I tell you, does not get destroyed. It separates from the dead body. That which leaves the body is the form of God. The knowledge 'I Am' is God. The knower of this God is a *Jnani*.

M: One believes in death due to ignorance. If death were a reality even in a single case, all the living beings would have died. A body is alive due to consciousness. Due to the separation of consciousness, the bodies can be said to have death. As you are the consciousness and not a body, you have no death.

The world has originated from a cause (consciousness) as small as an atom. Can you create a mountain from a mustard seed? But, it has actually happened. Hence, this world is false. Even then one has to behave properly and take care of oneself and one's dear ones. Taking this world as false, if one were to behave anyway one likes, that would lead to confusion and chaos. Despite all efforts there is so much misery in the world.

A life full of contentment is possible only after Self-realization. The evening talks begin at 5 p.m. and last until 6.30 pm. Without question and answers, one would find it very boring to spend this one and a half hour. Similarly, in this false world a true behaviour is advised. Even then, one must know what is true and what is false. And when one knows the why and how of our presence in this world, one's work is done.

The *Maya* or illusion shows us everything as false. But She herself is a cheat.

The world appears in the light of our beingness. Our beingness is also called as Ishwar or God.

Visitor: Why are we so unhappy?

M: Let us consider our dream experience. If a king sees himself as a beggar, can he be happy? Our condition is also similar even in this waking state. We do not know what we are. We believe ourselves to be that which, in reality, we are not. How can that lead to peace and tranquility? What is needed is correct knowledge and not more and more worldly acquisition.

V: Our worldly success gives temporary satisfaction.

M: A hundred years ago we did not know that we were, that we existed. Now, we know our presence. That is the blunder. We take our being as true. Our problems begin there. In Self-knowledge our beingness ends, with all its problems.

V: It is so nice to be in your presence.

M: You have been continuing your stay too much. You must also give others a chance. I tell you once again that you are not your body, but the dynamic consciousness (*Chaitanya Atma*). That is enough. Now, do not stay here any longer.

It is like getting your son married. Thereafter, how to increase his family and take care of it, is his business, not yours. Whatever is, is your knowledge 'I Am'. It is honest, it is dishonest. It is *Maya*, it is *Brahman*. Have you heard this? Now, that is enough. You may leave.

M: *Parabrahman*, the Absolute is desireless. What is the use of this beingness to It. One who knows the Truth remains aloof. Speachlessness befits the Great Man.

V: Can reading of sciptures help?

M: There is no end to reading scriptures and getting confused. In *Mahabharat*, the origin of Kauravas and Pandavas etc. confuse you more and more. Instead, know your beingness as light *(Bhagawan)* and Godly, and meditate on it. That would suffice. Your beingness is the seed of the world. It is your main capital. Take it with you and leave. I am pointing out to you, your greatest and the most valuable possession. Meditate on it and be free.

V: We are so thankful to you.

M: Some visitors take knowledge from us and with that they argue and quarrel with us. If that knowledge were their own, it would have been a different matter.

V: It is like giving a sword to a mad man.

M: In deep sleep, your feeling of false waking gives rise to a false dream world. How can a false thing give rise to something true? Similarly, the root of waking world is false. The root is 'I Am'. How can it give rise to a true world? Hence, this world is equally false.

※

December 13, 1979

TRANSCENDENCE FROM BECOMING AND BEING

ॐ

Maharaj: Have you taken the *Mantra*?

Visitor: Yes.

M: The *Mantra* reminds you of your true identity. Your parents gave you a certain name and all called you by that name. *Mantra* is called *Nama* (Name) *Mantra* i.e.calling yourself as you are in reality. This *Mantra* is very powerful and effective.

My Guru gave me this *Mantra* and the result is all these visitors from all over the world. That shows its power. There are different *Mantra*s. Every *Mantra* has a purpose, which is achieved by continuous chanting of the *Mantra*.

You do not know how your breathing takes place. Then, how difficult will it be to know the limitless. So far you have asked many people many things; and the net result is you are still in ignorance. One question you never asked anybody. That question is "whether you exist". You exist and that is your direct knowledge. You know it even in total darkness. Now, try to know yourself without asking anyone. Your capital is the knowledge 'you are'. Make use of it. Meditate on it, by it.

V: Can I use my own language, my mother tongue?

M: Meditation is without words.

From a flower a fruit appears and there are seeds in the fruit. Prior to the appearance of the flower something has happened in the plant for the appearance of the flower. For everyone, the first knowledge is of one's own existence. Thereafter, there is knowledge about others and there is beginning of activities. We act as per the meaning of the sounds that we hear. The listener of the sound is not in the body. The body is made of the quintessence of food. Its quality is our sense of being. The listener of sound is not the food body. He is the knower of consciousness.

M: (to a new visitor) : All this knowledge, what is its use to you?

V: To be free of ignorance.

M: With this knowledge one becomes free of all becoming, as well as of being. What remains to be done for him?

V: Nothing.

M: A *Jnani* becomes free of good and bad, profit and loss, birth and death. All the five elements take birth in the consciousness, into which they finally merge.

Some teachers declare consciousness as *Ishwara* or *Brahman* and that is what we are. But this is not the ultimate knowledge. This knowledge is in the field of *Maya* or illusion.

V: Do visions indicate spiritual progress?

M: One is able to see visions of Gods as per one's imagination. Prior to Self-realization, Sage Namdeo used to see God Vitthal in human form. Vitthal used to play and eat with Namdeo. For him it appeared to be the ultimate in spirituality. Other contemporary Sages like Jnaneshwar and Muktabai pointed out that Namdeo was not yet ripe to be a Sage. The Ultimate is beyond all forms. All experiences and visions are in the field of consciousness, which is the quality of food essence. One has to realize oneself as the knower of consciousness. If you stop eating, will you be conscious?

V: No.

M: While watching a dream, are you really awake?

V: No. But that is known after real waking.

M: If body is still your identity, it means all this knowledge has fallen on deaf ears.

In this world we come across poetic imagination and not Truth. None has time to go to the roots and to discover Truth.

Movies have become so popular and cinemas are overcrowed. What is there other than somebody's imagination?

Prophet Mohmad advocated polygamy for Muslims. The ratio of women to men was very high and it was necessary for every woman to get married. That would also help to increase the Muslim population.

All these happenings disturb our minds. A rare one tries to find answers from within oneself. One goes to the source of oneself. One is not the body which is only food material. The consciousness is the quality of food body. Hence, one is also not the consciousness. "What Am I without this consciousness?" to this question there is no reply. Even Vedas became silent at that point. The world is contained in a grain of food. How can it be true? With this observation one becomes aloof and unconcerned.

❧

PLAY OF FIVE ELEMENTS

We hear praise of a deity recited in benedictory verse at the beginning of a drama. In the verse there is some indication of the events that follow. Similarly, my present sickness (cancer) is indicative of the fullness that will be experienced in the near future.

M (to visitor): What is good for me, can you accept it boldly?

V: That is doubtful.

M: If you get eternal sleep, will you be happy?

V: (Silence.)

M: The events that happen, are they because of you or due to the five elements? How can you expect peaceful behaviour of the five elements? Whatever may happen, you have no part to play in it.

Because of your body identity, you experience happiness or unhappiness and you have to believe in birth and death.

All your organs of sensation is the function of the five elements. Your sense of being itself is the quality of the food essence, made of the five elements.

M: The word that you utter is the quality of space. Physical touch is the quality of air. Form is the quality of heat. Juice is the quality of water. And smell is the quality of the earth. Where are you in all these sense organs?

You may try to control the body made of the five elements; but how can you control the limitless five elements around you? For you there are the five sense organs; but the same are operating as the five elements outside.

The five elements come together to form the *sattva* or the

quintessence of food, in which there is your sense of being. Someone comes to know one's being. Who comes to know, cannot be said. The sense of being in human beings identifies with the body as its form. There are in all eighty four lakh different forms like worms, birds, animals etc. All forms are due to the five elements, all activities due to five elements. The existence of the 'me' in human beings as the doer, is imaginary.

When you come to know this reality all your worries will be over and all your identities will come to an end. The Absolute has no colour, no design, no name, no form. All the names and forms appear on the earth and all the imagination and writings are due to the consciousness in human form. The world is full of books containing concepts of their authors.

What we think ourselves to be, that goes on changing with time. From an infant to a child, to a boy, to a young man, to a middle aged to a very old man, our identity changes with time. No identity is steady and our knowledge about ourselves is valid only for that moment. Hence, what we think we are at any time, has no value. It is all meaningless. The identities are not ours but they are the states of food material, which contain somebody's sense of being. When 'I amness' goes, people call it death.

Knowing one's existence is miserable and it is a quality of the food body. When one does not know one's existence, that is in order and fine.

When you do not know 'you are' is there any fear?

V: There is no fear at all.

M: What I know myself to be, I am not that. I am That which I cannot know.

To go further, I am the soil, I am the stones. I am the food consumed. I am also that which is dropped in the toilet every morning. I am not an individual but the love and the feelings. Instead of calling the transient as untrue and a cheat, we call it *Maya*, the illusion.

We come across people who are confident that they know a lot. In my case, I know that I do not know anything.

Instead of saying that one lived for a hundred years, we should say, one suffered for a hundred years.

You are a witness to the events that happen around you. Identification leads to happiness or unhappiness. If there is no witnessing, will there be happiness or unhappiness? Without asking anyone, you can say that there was a time, when there was nothing to witness. This was your experience a hundred years ago. Hence, witnessing itself is a sin. The sin is not of an individual, but of the whole world.

An idol of stone, made by man, when worshipped gives you what you desire. This consciousness is much more powerful. When worshipped as God, it can give you anything.

For the earnest seekers, liberation is possible just by listening to this knowledge. There is no need to suffer by sacrifices and penance. All the false identities drop off and the ultimate remains in all its purity.

V: Then what should I do?

M: About that you need not worry now. Things will happen around you, as they need to happen.

❧

December 14, 1979

'I DO NOT KNOW',
IS THE BEST STATE OF BEING

Visitor: I have solved all my riddles except the one of the Self.

Maharaj: When you look at you as you are, no riddle will remain. Do you have direct knowledge of your birth?

V: No.

M: After your so called birth your hunger and thirst started, naturally, so also urination and excretion. It was not your doing. Your knowing contains everything. If there is no knowingness, there is nothing.

Your knowledge 'you are' or your consciousness is a store house of all visible forms. Your whole world is in it. Your memory 'you are' identifies with the body. But that memory has no form. If you call it *Atma* or Self, the Self has no form.

Have you given a thought to your true identity?

V: I try to remind myself of my true being.

M: If you are not your body and its name, what are you?

V: (Silence.)

M: Let the body be there. Only, do not identify with it. "I do not know" is the best attitude. We cannot point out Reality as this or as that. We can only say *"neti, neti"* which means "not this, not this".

When you will realize the Self, there will be no need to repeat "I am not this body". Then you make use of the body as an instrument.

M: In deep sleep are you aware of the body?

V: No.

M: Identification with the body arises after waking. When a seeker comes to know that his consciousness is composed of all the five elements and the three qualities, what can you say about his worthiness. Those, whom we call as incarnations, they had the same consciousness as you have now. The world takes birth in your consciousness.

V: There are social reformers in this world, who do so much for the people.

M: Yes. They do good work. If we start counting the number of living beings born on this earth so far, what will be your number?

V: (Silence.)

M: When did you hear the first word or sentence in your life? Then, how old were you? How old are you now?

V: Fifty.

M: Not much. Did you know your parents fifty one years ago? We give a thought to our existence only after the beingness appears and not before.

Some people assume themselves to be all powerful. But do we have any definite identity, which can do anything without failure? In this world, could any one do any reforms, which lasted indefinitely?

M: In our childhood, we followed our parents and did whatever they told us. Now, your Guru tells you that you have no name and form and that you are free, right at this moment. Why not take it?

There are stages of one's evolution. One speaks as one understands. One's talk is correct for that stage in which one is. When one really understands, one knows that one was never born. Then one cannot ask questions about the date and time of one's birth. When there is no birth, how can death arise?

V: Is there knowledge 'I Am' in food material?

M: The food juices do not have the knowledge 'I Am'; but when the same become the body of a human being, the knowledge 'I Am' begins. Thereafter, the suffering and the struggle for survival also begin. It is natural for the 'I love' to struggle to exist. When the sense of being unknowingly appears in a form, the so called birth takes place.

V: Is suffering avoidable?

M: The happenings or the events flow from the consciousness and the imaginary somebody or some being which feels its individual existence, suffers because of them. The food body has form, but the behaviour is formless.

The knowledge 'I Am' is the quality of *sattva* or food essence and the waking and sleep states accompany it. When the food body becomes old the sense organs and the organs of action become weak and they do not function properly.

Anybody's sense of being has no form or name. But one assumes the form of the food body as one's own form and accepts the name given to it. The happening of good and bad are all concepts, as there is none to whom they can happen.

In ignorance, one believes in one's real existence and presence. This habit is formed since childhood and the same cannot leave easily.

Distant invisible stars are made visible by a telescope. Your consciousness is like the telescope, due to which many things become visible. Observation is the quality of the consciousness and not of the observer. Witnessing of the consciousness happens to the observer. The consciousness contains everything. Witnessing of all that happens to the observer.

M (to Visitor): The talks that are going on now, whose quality is it?

V: It is the quality of the consciousness.

M: From wheat and rice, how many different types of food items can you make?

V: Innumerable.

M: Similarly, there is no end to the happenings in consciousness. What is birth?

V: It is the appearance of 'I Am' consciousness.

M: All are qualities of the consciousness and not of the witness of consciousness. The consciousness occupies the whole universe and is called *Vishwambhara.* Innumerable people and other living beings lived in the last three ages. What happened to them? How are they now?

V: They died long ago.

M: I know how they are now. All of them are like you, what you were before taking this form. All your riddles will get solved as soon as you know the "why and how" of your consciousness. You know that your consciousness was not there (a hundred years ago). Now it is there. The "Why and how" of it, you must know. It is your business to know it. Who else will know it and tell you?

Now, I am talking. To whom, am I telling all this? I am not talking to men and women. I am talking to the birth principle. The forms have appeared after the so called birth.

You are unable to participate in these talks, since you have no knowledge. Who has knowledge here? Is it a joke to convince these foreign visitors?

Seekers get confused by hearing different statements at different times. "Yesterday, he said that. Today he is telling totally different." **Although I am talking to pure consciousness (birth principle),** the listeners are men and women. Hence, the misunderstanding and confusion.

M: The food material is not a living being. If a donkey eats it, the material becomes a donkey. If a monkey eats it, it becomes a monkey. The birth principle is not a product of imagination, but you (man or woman) are. Then how can there be proper understanding?

In existence, there is nothing smaller or nothing greater than consciousness. All of you experience it as your 'I Am'. In the field of consciousness, there are infinite names, but the witness of consciousness has no name.

When we talk to others, we use words of our choice. Others use words of their choice. If there is disagreement about the words used, there is quarrel and even a fight. Words give rise to harsher words and the wise one requests all to stop talking And there is silence and peace.

The world functions with the understanding that all bodies and the world are real. In reality, both are false and that is true understanding. The bodies and the world are made of the same five elements. One who sees oneself as apart from the food body, is already free.

The Absolute is nameless, but in trying to understand, we use names like *Paramatma* or *Parabrahman*.

M: The people who visit me find it difficult to understand me. It would be an achievement even if a single person out of a group would correctly understand me.

What you see, this world is nothing other than the forms taken by the imagination of the human intellect. The world has been made beautiful by the ideas flowing out in a human form. The concept 'I Am' in human form has great powers. But identification with the body has resulted in the tragedy of death.

V: Everything is so real. How is it an illusion?

M: From the Absolute standpoint, all is *Maya*, an illusion.

V: What is the power of consciousness?

M: Just as there is fire in this towel, but it is not seen, there are great powers and abilities in this consciousness.

V: How did the sense of being appear from the Eternal?

M: Our sense of being is the content of the womb. It is dormant in the womb and it continues to be so upto three to five years after delivery. It is like a raw mango which takes time to become sweet. When your beingness attained maturity you started recognising your mother. This being is very ancient and eternal, but was without the sense of being. The sense of being appeared only after the availability of a food body. The condition of our being upto the age of three to five is the same as that of the Eternal.

V: Why has the Truth become so difficult to realize?

M: Truth is available to all, but it remains hidden. An ant picks up a sugar crystal covered by sand. You have to take Guru's help to locate Truth and realize it. The Truth becomes open and free, when all the heard and read concepts are blown away.

V: Why is the Sage so rare to find?

M: It is said that one who realizes the Self, hides it. In reality there is no hiding. As there are no real customers for Truth, the Sage appears to hide It. A rare one seeks Truth. Others are after the things of the world. They worship God for material gains. A Sage is full of patience to wait for the rare seeker. Sage Jnaneshwar has said that the knowledge is imparted as per the capacity of the listener.

V: What is *Maya*?

M: When we come to know we are, we like it and we want to sustain it. That is *Maya*.

V: Why is there confusion and chaos in the world?

M: The real waking is to realize the Self. This (your) waking is as good as the dream waking. You do not expect anything from your dream world, as it is false. But this world is as false as the dream world. You take it as true and expect to be benefited. Until you realize your Self, there will be no order in your world.

V: Why is our waking false?

M: The knowledge 'you are' is the seed of the world that you see. The dream 'you are' gives rise to your dream world and the waking 'you are' gives rise to this world. As 'you are' itself is an illusion, both the worlds are false. I do not experience the world through books. The world is my direct experience. It is the qualify of my 'I Am' knowledge. I exist, hence I see my world. The world is made of the five elements. These elements do not follow any guidelines. They are free to behave as they like. Hence, the world is as it is.

V: I should not have taken birth in such a world.

M: In a moment, billions and billion of births take place. Whose births are they? You give names as per the body forms. But, all of them are appearances of consciousness in food bodies of eighty four lakh different types of species from the amoeba to a human being. All these forms vanish but not the consciousness, which is deathless.

V: Why are there so many religions?

M: One likes one's own concepts and wants others to follow them. If this succeeds one gets followers. This leads to creeds and religions.

December 15, 1979

THE ETERNAL
IS SPEAKING HERE

Maharaj: The human body, as well as, all other living forms are made of the food essence in which the five elements are present. The activities happen due to the three *gunas* or qualities. Can you point out even a single body in which the elements are absent?

Visitor: No. That is not possible.

M: Even the incarnations of Ram or Krishna cannot be an exception to this.

Every element is measureless and unlimited. To consider a separate existence to every living form or an individual is imaginary.

Your world exists when you know you are. In deep sleep you do not know you are and there is no world.

We are the outcome of the food juices on this earth. Is earth knowledgeable?

V: No.

M: You are the dust to which you ultimately return. People come here to get their problems solved. Perhaps people come here when their problems are nearing their ends.

V: Does *Maya* exist after Self-realization?

M: For a Sage, it does not matter whether She exists or not. A sick man was advised to drink the mixture after rubbing air on space for three days.

Is there knowledge in anybody's words in this world.

(Silence.)

M: People who come here may complain that they did not receive any knowledge but were more confused.

The Eternal is speaking here, making use of words. The Eternal is not a part of the transient.

V: Do people suffer as per their belief?

M: If people express their confidence that something evil is going to happen to them, I tell them that it is their destiny, which I cannot change.

For me it is enough to realize that I am not a part of that which comes and goes, which rises and sets.

V: If I am not the body, what are my limits?

M: I tell the seekers not to underestimate themselves. You are so big that one will find it difficult to get a rope long enough to encircle you.

In other words, one will take ages to go round you and still be unable to complete the circle. Better leave this place at the earliest, before you lose all your belief about yourself.

That which says anything, is always the consciousness and about what is said, is the expression of consciousness.

V: Every moment there are billions and billions of births.

M: Who are born?

V: Human beings, animals etc.

M: No. All are the births of consciousness in various forms. Just as the embryo remains hidden, the Cosmic egg (*Hiranyagarbha*) also remains hidden.

There are scientists doing great inventions. There are astronauts going into space to study distant planets. When these great men study themselves, what will they find?

V: Nothing.

M: The knowledge of the scientists is material knowledge. Our knowledge 'we are' is also due to food material. So far these scientists have not succeeded in creating human beings directly from food material. For that the union of the male and the female is required.

V: Are you confident to face any question?

M: When people from all over the world visit me, I have nothing to worry. One, who was born, will only be visiting. The unborn cannot come. And what is born, is very well known to me. I know how the consciousness has appeared and where it is situated.

December 16, 1979

YOUR NEED TO EXIST, MADE YOU LIMITED
ꙮ

Maharaj: Things are as they are. One flower is as it is and the other as it is. What further examination do you need there?

(Silence.)

M: First, the consciousness appeared and then all these scenes. In the scene, different forms appear at different times. Right from an ant to human beings, the activities happen as per the flow of thoughts. The consciousness in every form is time bound. When the time is over it disappears.

Just as you see grass and new plants coming up in rainy season, there is creation of living beings of various types.

The human suffering is due to concepts, which may differ from actual facts. A man is guided and directed by the flow of thoughts from within. Thereby, some unimportant person may become a great historical figure.

Visitor: That is true. Without the inner guidance, we would not have done anything.

M: It is the consciousness that listens to the Guru and not your mind. Give attention to your consciousness. Meditate on it as Guru, as God, as *Brahman*. The universe and all the ten directions rise from it. You must realize this truth, yourself.

M: Do as you are told and your spiritual progress and material sustenance, will be looked after well. A rare one realises the truth of this. I am the same as you are. The difference is only in the realization. You are equally eligible to attain It.

V: We have our limitations.

M: You take yourself as an individual, which you are not. I know myself as manifest and boundless. When 'I Am', the creation, sustenance and the dissolution are also there. But I am That which has no birth and no death.

The five elements are present in all living forms. To give an example, the air or vital breath is present in all beings. I am That or that is mine, which is common in all. You can call it *Brahman*. I am not an individual but indivisible or present in all. The qualities of five elements are my own qualities. All these qualities make the nature (*Nisarga*). All the incarnations happen in nature. All are one with the five elements and have an individual form. For you all the forms of men and women are real. For Me even *Prakriti* and *Purusha* are formless. You give different names to various forms; but you agree that without forms all are one.

All forms are time bound. As compared to the infinite, any time duration is so short, as if zero. Hence, all forms are only glimpses and illusory. They have only momentary appearance.

From the standpoint of a Sage, a child which is born and the one before conception, both belong to the same class. A momentary appearance merges with the eternal disappearance. There are differences in appearance, but unity in disappearance. Even dreams appear and disturb. Are they real?

V: No. I am glad to know from you, what God is.

M: No. All this is your information, What are you in reality? My Guru told me what I am. The same I tell you. Do you agree?

V: Yes.

M: The world that I see is my own expression. All the information I get about this world, is my own information. For you that man and that woman are different. Even a man acting as a woman in a drama, does not forget that he is a man. For me all are myself. All names and forms are my own.

Brahman is neither a man nor a woman. It is formless. You notice the form and forget the content, the Reality. All the five elements are responsible for any form. To consider oneself as a man or as a woman, is a kind of sickness. When you hear these talks, you see yourself as infinite and boundless. You cannot be restricted to a small body. Slowly see yourself as wider and wider. You will soon realize that due to sickness of identification with the body, you have become a man or a woman. It is not a question of telling others what you are, but having the inner conviction about your true nature.

A rare one like Krishna will see Himself as He is and tell others about it. In *Gita* He has made it very clear. He sees Himself in the world and all is His information. All these names like Shiva, Ram and Krishna are the names of nature (*Nisarga*) personified. These names depict the behaviour of nature.

Just as the qualities of each of the five elements differ from those of others, in nature we see different qualities. When you cannot change a child, you admit that its qualities are such that they cannot be changed.

All the functioning of the universal family is due to *Prakriti* and *Purusha*. The *Purusha* is only a witness and it is all the work of *Prakriti*.

A true disciple says, "When death is unavoidable, why not do as Guru says and see what happens?" A great devotee treats God as his friend and says to Him, "Everything belongs to you and it is going to remain with you only. Why do you doubt that I will take a part of it?"

M: I have observed life as it is and taken lessons from it. Our existence in any form is most unreliable. Our close relative who is with us today, may not be there tomorrow. The only son of parents may lie dead in front of them.

This is the nature of existence, which we cannot change. We can only change ourselves, to get the least affected by these mishaps. The unreliability teaches us to be detached. Nothing should be able to disturb our peace and tranquility. I have made practical use of these uncertainties of life.

So far, I have told you the side which is known. The other side, of which you do not have any direct knowledge, is the Truth. The first is with consciousness (*Saguna*) and the other is non-conscious (*Nirguna*), devoid of all attributes. The conscious appears to be unlimited but it is transitory and untruth. The non-conscious appears to be little. Still it is Eternal and hence, the Truth.

My need to exist made me limited. My incompleteness increased in direct proportion to my need. When there was no need to exist, I was unlimited, True and Eternal.

That, which is not known directly, that is the Truth. That state of mine, about which I cannot say anything, That is in perfect order. The manifest is transitory and the unmanifest (*Nirguna*) is the Eternal and That is the Truth.

V: The spirituality also teaches us how to live in this world.

M: Yes. Do not love the transitory, if you desire peace and tranquility. Love the Eternal, if you can. At least love your 'I Am'. Make friendship with it. It will never leave you alone. It will give you lifelong Company. It is the nearest and the best Godly Companion. It is the most reliable.

December 17, 1979

ALL INDIVIDUALS
ARE IMAGINARY

Maharaj: There is no life without the five elements. All the so called individuals owe their existence to the five elements. All objects are made of two or more of the five elements. Only when the elements come together to form *sattva* or food essence, there is the sense of being or the *Atma* (Self). Although all living forms are time-bound, some forms like that of Markandeya have very long lives.

In nature and consciousness there is no law and order. Man desires order, but has no control over nature. Hence, he assumes law and order in nature.

The five elements, three qualities, *Prakriti* and *Purusha* all these are formless. All forms made of these ten have imaginary existence.

I am getting my taste 'I Am'. It was not there a hundred years back. But now it is there. My first job is to find out the "why and how" of this taste.

M: In this search for the Truth, I found out that my 'I' had no existence. I found out that this 'I' was not individual but the

'Universal I'. The real 'I' was of the entire existence, without any individuality. With this finding, my search ended there. What existed was not 'I' but *Brahman*. You feel that your existence is important. Hence, everything is important to you. If your existence loses its importance, nothing has any importance to you.

You know 'you are' and you want to exist always. You want company of your body, indefinitely. But it is a food body which has ageing and time limit. How can it remain healthy forever?

Every human being appears to be made of two ends. The first is an assumed end, the beginning of 'I Am' and the second is the active end, which works for the sustenance of the first end. Without the first, the second has no meaning. The second depends upon the first and sustains it. The second works as long as the first is.

As all individuals are imaginary, it is wrong to criticize the family affairs of anybody. In reality it is the affair of the Entire – the *Brahman*. The astral body occupies the whole of existence. Although we restrict ourselves to the body, that is not our actual experience. We always experience everything around us, in which our body also exists. This applies to the waking, as well as the dream states. That's why it appears as if we are trying to force ourselves to be bodies, against our actual experience which is otherwise. It is not an individual who experiences the entire, but it is the entire, the manifest, that experiences the entire. Every being is not separate, but it is always with the group of ten – five elements, three *gunas*, *Prakriti* and *Purusha*.

Visitor: Is it possible to impart knowledge without words?

M: The use of words is to help you to understand. Your ignorance is due to the words heard and read. My words are meant to wipe out those words. Some visitors make use of words to argue. Proper understanding leads to less and less words, and more and more silence.

V: How does meditation on knowledge 'I Am' help?

M: Other than your body and the sense of being, what is your capital in this world? Without asking anybody, what is your direct knowledge? You know 'you are' and the world, in which your body exists. You have no direct knowledge of God or *Brahman*.

Your 'I Am' knowledge comes first and then the world. Hence, your 'I Am' knowledge should get the first place in importance. You know that this 'I Am' knowledge was absent a hundred years back. Now it is there. It is your first duty to find out the 'why and how' of this 'I Am' appearance. Other things of lesser importance can be investigated later. Meditation on 'I Am' is done to be free of words and thoughts.

In this cigarette lighter the flame is sustained by the burning gas. Similarly, your consciousness is sustained by digestion of the food you eat. We see the body eating; but the beneficiary is the light of consciousness or the light of knowledge 'I Am'.

V: After Self-realization, what happens to the bondage?

M: One sees it as illusory. He sees himself as a great Sun illuminating all existence. Until then, one is wrapped up in the concepts of one's own mind. All ignorance and bondage is due to the heard and read knowledge. Be in the state prior to hearing anything. In that state prior to consciousness, there was no unhappiness and hence no need to be happy. Your knowingness is the seed of misery, which gives rise to your world, full of unhappiness.

❧

December 18, 1979

VERY FEW DOUBT THE CONTENT OF SCRIPTURES

Visitor: How was our existence prior to the appearance of our beingness?

Maharaj: It was unmanifest, as if it did not exist. Its appearance was like the sudden appearance of a plant in rainy season. If I ask you which way did the plant travel to appear there. For the plant, there is no question of coming there by any path. It was there only, but unmanifest. There only it manifested.

V: What about the law of *karma*?

M: Birth, rebirth and the law of *karma* are all concepts based on the ignorance of Truth.

When all forms are imaginary, whose *karma* (action) and whose birth/rebirth can it be? If one had a true concrete form, one would suffer in the same form due to one's actions.

The law of *karma* is based on the assumption that all forms are real and a record of all actions is maintained. Although all forms are false, what is true in them are the five elements. These elements can be held responsible for the actions and should be punished to the extent as they deserve it.

V: How has untruth got established as the Truth?

M: In scriptures there are additions by unauthorised writers. Most of them are ignorant people, whose books would have been ignored in normal course. Hence, these writers indicated the names of Vyasa etc. as the author, for easy acceptance by people.

Also, there are very few who question the content of the scriptures. They are taken for granted as the Truth. Even if it is not, it does not matter. For the common man spirituality comes last in their list of priorities. There are other important matters like supply of food, rising prices, political instability etc. which need immediate attention. Spirituality can wait until one gets very old. Hence, as years pass doubtful untruth gets established as the Truth.

V: If all forms are unreal, there is no question of any coming and going or birth and rebirth.

M: The world is full of people and the population is ever increasing. Wherefrom are they coming? They appear and multiply there only. They are going to disappear there only.

All living beings are free to act. There is no force of any kind to reproduce. The multiplication of food bodies is happening spontaneously.

V: Sage Tukaram has said, "I was in *Vaikuntha* (the abode of God Vishnu) and I have come from there."

M: If I meet him I will question him.

M: Where were you in *Vaikuntha*?

Vaikuntha and *Kailas* (the abode of God Shiva) are very popular concepts, where the meritorious are supposed to land after departure from here.

We have come to know our existence here only, on this earth and we are going to disappear here only. Where is the question of going to or coming from *Vaikuntha* or *Kailas*?

Just as we add the prefix of Late for the departed, Hindus add the prefix of *Vaikunthavasi* (residing in *Vaikuntha*) or *Kailasvasi* (residing in *Kailas*).

The time when you first came to know 'you are' and the place, where it was known, these tell you the time and place of your manifestation. There is no question of your coming from anywhere else. The same way, you merge with the unmanifest, when your 'I amness' is no more.

V: Does a *Jnani* make use of His intellect?

M: You make use of your intellect for your sustenance. For the knower of intellect, sustenance happens spontaneously.

V: Like that of the embryo?

M: Yes. He is truly independent (*Swatantra*) and Self supporting. One whose stress is on 'I' as the doer, has a long way to go; but one who stabilizes prior to 'I', attains the Self. One has to go back to the state, when 'I Am' was absent. That state is in perfect order.

Every one comes to know that one is, through the food juices; but ultimately who is it, that comes to know? In order to understand, you give him a name e.g. Absolute. It means, it is the Absolute which comes to know that 'It is'. Sri Krishna was an expression of the Absolute. During His lifetime, He said so many things; *Bhagavad Gita* is His song, but the Absolute remains free of words and untouched by them.

V: Are other animals affected by concepts?

M: Man accumulates concepts by hearing and reading. In the absence of intellect, other animals don't have that capacity.

V: Did Krishna's devotees (*gopis*) remember Him, after His death?

M: During Krishna's lifetime itself, the *gopis* had lost their individuality and had become one with Krishna. Hence, this question doesn't arise. When the news 'I Am' goes, what remains is the no-news (*Nivrutta*) state.

December 19, 1979

MIND – INDICATOR
NOT DICTATOR

Maharaj: I am in my True state, the Absolute. Although I am not restricted to this body, it will indicate my whereabouts. That will continue till the end of the body. In my Eternal state, there is existence without the news 'I Am'.

V: How will you describe our life?

M: It is full of mental modifications and on the look out for entertainment. Just as you know the presence of a dead rat by its smell, currently you are smelling your own presence. But this smelling is time-bound and it is going to vanish. A hundred years back, you did not smell your presence. It has started after the so called birth. What has started, has also to stop one day, at the so called death.

Prior to smelling your presence, what were your desires and demands? There has been no end to your desires and acquisitions, now.

V: How is the mind related to the vital breath?

M: Mind is another name for the vital breath.

There is air in the atmosphere, and there is breathing in and out. Due to this the vital breath functions. This results in the flow of thoughts, which we call as mind. The ignorant functions as per the flow of thoughts.

V: Does a *Jnani* have a mind?

M: It is there but very feeble and distant. Just as you are not disturbed by some minor events in Russia, no thoughts affect a *Jnani*.

V: Do you ignore mind totally?

M: Its intimation is accepted for matters like going to toilet etc. A *Jnani*'s mind has no say. It serves only as an indicator and not a dictator. Mind dictates the ignorant. Just now we saw a person, who was sitting here quietly, suddenly got up and left. Who told him to leave?

V: His mind.

M: Man feels that he is the decider and the doer. He forgets that he, along with all living beings, is a part of the five elements. What happens amongst the five elements, finally lands on the earth, of which man is a part. Man has to act as per the result of the interaction between all the elements.

V: Does a Guru know this interaction?

M: One who knows proper action and that action, which should be avoided, is a Guru.

V: If our very being is the quality of the food essence, we cannot expect to have any control over our actions.

M: Our sense of being is like a season, which has a beginning and also an end. Our being is important to us and we take all precautions and we work regularly for its sustenance.

V: What spiritual practices do you recommend?

M: Try to live separating yourself from the body and its name.

If you are not the body and its name, what are you? Although you take yourself as an individual, your 'I Am' knowledge is the Yoga (union) of the five elements and the three qualities. It is a Yoga of eight (five + three) limbs or *Ashtanga* (eight limb) Yoga.

V: Why do I find it difficult to remain without any physical or mental activity?

M: Because you want to forget your beingness, which is troublesome. In deep sleep, you are comfortable as your beingness is forgotten.

V: How to be free of this trouble?

M: Know your beingness i.e. the 'why and how' of it.

V: How to know it?

M: Meditate on your beingness i.e. be without thoughts and your beingness itself will tell you all its secrets.

V: My body formation happened without my knowledge and permission. What can you say about its end?

M: The end may be with your knowledge, but it will again be without your consent. Even God (*Ishwara*) has an end.

V: What is the importance of the *Mahat Tatwa* or the Supreme Consciousness?

M: Just as all your property is because of your money power, all your existence is due to this *Mahat Tatwa* or *Shuddha* (pure) *Sattva*. When the light of *Sattva* sets, it is all over. Your world is the quality of *Sattva*.

V: Who is *Vasudeo*?

M: *Vas* means smell. You know your being. It means you smell your being, because of your consciousness. Consciousness is God (*Deo*). The light or *Bhagwan* is in the body, as long as you smell your being. When consciousness separates from the body, the smelling stops. Nothing dies.

V: What is self-love?

M: What is born is self-love. You want to live at any cost. You love to exist. Self-love is your main capital.

V: Does a *Jnani* have self-love?

M: A *Jnani* is one, who knows the origin of self-love. He has no self-love. Ignorance sustains self-love. The ignorant suffers so much due to self-love. All our activities including Yoga, meditation and penance for Self-realization are due to self-love. *Maya* is self-love. As long as you love to live, you cannot get rid of *Maya*. You are not a director, but only a helpless actor of your life-show.

V: How to get rid of this ignorance?

M: You cannot remove it by effort. It goes when you know its cause.

V: Why are only a few interested in Self-knowledge?

M: The urge must come from within. When people find out that their material achievements cannot give much, their spiritual quest begins. The futility of wealth cannot come to the poor. Hence, Indians have a long way to go to turn to spirituality. A considerable number, who come here are for their worldly problems. The visitors from Europe and U.S.A. are ever increasing.

V: How to get rid of this body identity?

M: You must remember the fact that you are infinite and boundless. By training and habit you have imagined yourself to be limited to the body. Your imaginary somebody, is troubled by problems. In the case of a *Jnani* there is no somebody to suffer.

V: This continuous talk must be strenuous for Maharaj.

M: This corpse (my body) is burning round the clock. Doctors advise me to stop talking and take medicines. But what do they know? For me, the remedy will be worse than the disease. There is no pain, but only weakness. I have no energy to sit; but as soon as I sit in front of you, I start talking.

V: Our sense of being is so small, but it contains vast space.

M: When Krishna said, "I am everything", he meant His 'I amness' is everything. This is everybody's experience.

Even when Krishna was very young, many yogis and Mahatmas visited him seeking his advice and blessings.

V: Incarnations like Ram and Krishna did so much for the world.

M: But did any reforms last for a long time? Could they or anybody else stop the cycles of creation, sustenance and destruction? Could they control the five elements?

V: Some great men declared that they would come again at such and such a place.

M: I will not say that; because all forms are my own forms and all that is seen is my expression.

V: We see dead bodies. Then, how do you say that there is no death?

M: All bodies are made of five elements, and they are alive because of the consciousness. When consciousness separates, there is no life in the bodies. The consciousness does not die, but only separates from the bodies. Without consciousness the bodies were dead only. Then who dies there?

The consciousness serves as an instrument, because of which witnessing happens to the Absolute. Without consciousness the Absolute cannot witness anything.

M: The Absolute first witnesses the consciousness, when it exists and then witnesses its content. If the consciousness is called *Brahman*, its witness is *Parabrahman*.

M *(To a new visitor):* How many years are you doing your spiritual practices?

V: For over twelve years.

M: Do you know that this consciousness was not there... say, a hundred years ago?

V: Yes.

M: Your beingness is time-bound. It has a beginning and also an end. For the Absolute and also for the consciousness, there is no coming and going. The consciousness appears and at the end, it separates from the body. The witnessing happens to the Absolute and then it stops happening, when the consciousness separates from the body.

V: What is the use of all my spiritual knowledge?

M: Without knowing the "why and how" of the transition from the no-knowing state to the knowing state, all knowledge is useless.

When your plane landed in India, you know the arrival time. Similarly, what was your arrival time in this life?

V: It is the date and time of my birth.

M: No. It is the time of your conception. That is the real arrival and not the delivery time. Do you know wherefrom you arrived?

V: No. It happened without my knowledge.

M: Your state was the same prior to conception, during conception and about three years after the conception. You came to know about your arrival, three to five years after delivery.

At conception, your presence was dormant, like the

presence of fire in this towel. The child starts knowing its presence after it begins to recognise its mother.

V: Can fire burn this consciousness?

M: No. It can burn only the body. Consciousness separates from the body. Self is indestructible and deathless. Self-knowledge is to know your state prior to conception.

V: What is our true identity?

M: It is That which does not change with time. All our identities have changed with time. Is not all our knowledge about ourselves meaningless?

V: All our memories are photographic. Any past scene in our life, when recalled, it appears in front of us in the form of a photograph.

M: Have you taken these pictures? They happen automatically. All our activities go on smoothly, because of these photographs. You can recognise people and places visited by you earlier.

V: How do we recognise a person hearing his voice?

M: That also gets recorded.

V: What is the use of chanting *Guru-Mantra*?

M: For overall purification including that of the five *Pranas* (vital breaths). Although vital breath is only one, it is sub-divided into five *Pranas*, as per their functions. The pure seeker realizes the Self.

V: Why are real seekers very few in number?

M: Only a few have the inner urge. It cannot be developed externally. One who receives the divine grace of the Self, meets one's Sadguru. First there is *Atmakrupa* grace of the Self, then *Gurukrupa* grace of Guru and finally Self-realizatoin.

V: Is *Atma* (Self) one or many in different forms?

M: *Atma* is one only, but it expresses as 'I Am' in different forms. All the five elements come together for this sense of being to appear. For Self-realization one must hug 'I Am' by itself, i.e. to remain without thoughts. That is called meditation. Forgetting the world, to hold its Soul i.e. 'I Am'.

V: Everybody appears to have a separate *Atma*.

M: The same lake supplies water to people of Mumbai. Water is one, but when it fills the tanks in different buildings, everybody says it is his water.

V: How will you describe the Truth and untruth, in short.

M: What you cannot know is the Truth, and what you can know, but which changes, is the untruth.

V: To be born, is to suffer. Can we remain unborn?

M: You cannot stop that, which happens without your knowledge.

V: At least, God should stop it.

M: All living forms, including those of Ram and Krishna, are the products of *Nisarga* (nature). God has not created this universe. One living form is the food of another living form. Is it not cruelty? Even we do our best to stop cruelty. Is God so cruel as to do all this? Such a creator should be either an idiot or a demon.

There is so much destruction due to natural calamities. If God has created this universe, he would have taken care to control the five elements. As there is no creator, the elements are free to act, without control.

V: If not God, at least *Brahman* or *Parabrahman* should do something.

M: All these names are given only for better understanding. There are no forms corresponding these names. The creation of all living forms is like cooking a pancake on a hot plate. Their destinies are as per the quality of the food essence (*Sattva*) at the time of creation. One will become a beggar and another a king, as per the quality. One, who cannot be described by words and who is beyond space, is a *Jnani*. He has no name and form.

V: The appearance of 'I taste' is birth and its disappearance is death. Where will the taste go after death?

M: This flame of the gas lighter, where will it go when extinguished? It will vanish where it appeared from. There is no coming and going. The heaven and hell are the ideas devised by the wise to make people behave properly.

V: How can I be sure that there is God?

M: Do you have any doubt about your existence?

V: No.

M: You know you are because of your consciousness. I tell you that your consciousness is God. To doubt His existence, is to doubt your own. Your consciousness contains the whole world.

You will come across many who say that Krishna is their soul. But I tell you that I am Krishna's soul.

V: How to know It?

M: You must find out your Eternal nature. Then, you will know that you, as well as God, do not exist. It has happened in my case. First *Ishwara* died and then... (Maharaj pointed his finger to himself). You know whatever God knows and God knows whatever you know. When all my knowledge vanishes, God also becomes blank.

V: Many are getting interested in God.

M: That is because of the uncertainty in life and fear. When you truly understand the qualities of *sattva*, *rajas* and *tamas*, all your fear will go. Your 'I Am' is the quality of these three. They have no death, then, how can you die? Not knowing 'you are', cannot be called death. It happens in deep sleep as well. Are you dead?

V: Why am I not this body?

M: This body, which is made of the five elements, is a part of the universe. When you are not the five elements, how can you be the body? That body contains the news that you exist. You cannot be the news.

V: I am never alone even in a dream. When 'I Am' is everything, is it possible to be alone without anybody or anything?

M: That is possible only when your 'I Am' vanishes. Then, there would be no others or no other things. That is a non-dual state.

V: Sometimes we become happy or unhappy because of others.

M: The existence of others depends upon you. A hundred years ago, when you were not, all were absent. In deep sleep also everything vanishes. All that, which depends upon you, should not give you happiness or unhappiness. Your existence does not depend upon others.

V: Do you have death?

M: Have I remained without death? Having died, I am alive. I see everybody as myself – pure and complete. But they hold on to their beliefs and suffer. What can I do?

M: How do I look at anybody? I look at one, as one was prior to conception. But everyone considers oneself as per one's concepts. According to that one suffers. The Eternal does not need medicines to exist and to survive.

V: There is happiness or unhappiness only after birth.

M: Birth means the appearance of the three states of waking, sleep and knowingness; and the behaviour is by the three qualities of *Sattva*, *Rajas* and *Tamas*. Where are you in all these? You imagine yourself to be there and suffer. Happiness or unhappiness is only an imagination, of the imaginary.

All one's actions serve to provide relief from sorrow. One cries, or shouts or abuses others in anger. All these actions help to calm one's mind.

V: Even sickness can be imagined.

M: Many a times people come to me with some physical problems. I tell them, "There is nothing wrong with you. Forget it. Nothing can happen to you. And these people are cured without medicines. It is faith healing.

M (**to a new visitor**) : You are confident that 'you are'. On what does this confidence depend?

V: It is very clear from your talks.

M: If you really know it, you become deathless.

Let us consider an oil lamp. *Sattva* is the light, in which activities happen due to *Rajas*. And the soot on the glass bulb of the lamp is *Tamas*.

December 20, 1979

Your Concepts Have Clouded The Self

Maharaj: Regarding the Self, I give you important, useful hints. Its realization is your job. Parents will help their son to get married. Thereafter what to do is his job and not parents. Listening to this knowledge is to die while living. It is the death of your identity, which doesn't leave the ignorant till end. The timid leave a Sage, out of fear of extinction.

One is so much attached to the body that one finds it impossible to accept even a separation from the body. It almost amounts to the death of the body. For a true seeker the body is only a cause of the question, "What am I?" He has no doubt about his existence apart from the body.

V: Can I know or observe my death?

M: Death happens when the sense of being vanishes permanently. Without the sense of being how will you know death? You go to sleep every day. If there is no waking in or after sleep, it is death. The difference between sleep and death is only the fear about the latter. For a *Jnani* the clearing of the vital breath is blissful, similar to your happiness in the toilet, every morning.

V: If I do not get sleep, I take a pill.

M: Similarly, knowingness, waking and sleep are the result of a big pill called food essence. What is birth, other than, the appearance of these three states. Their disappearance is death.

V: Who is fit to receive spiritual knowledge?

M: One, who is distressed by physical, mental and spiritual problems.

V: If I do not get liberated in this life, will I die?

M: Knowingness, waking and sleep are the qualities of the food essence. Are you the food you eat?

V: No.

M: Your body is your food, not you. Its death is not your death. Thereafter, your knowingness will be no more. A hundred years back, your knowingness was absent. Were you dead?

V: No. If there is no death whether I am realized or not, why take all the trouble?

M: Only verbal knowledge, without realization, cannot remove fear. You cannot fill your stomach, by reading breakfast menu card. The knowledge is defined as That which liberates. It brings peace and tranquility. The load which you carry on your head will then be put on your table.

V: When one is no more, who is there to receive the offerings made to the departed?

M: None. Those who make the offerings, get satisfaction and the priest, his fee (*dakshina*).

V: Now, I am free of most of my concepts.

M: Your concepts, based on hearsay, have clouded the Self. This knowledge should be able to free you even of your 'I Am', which is also a concept. Your Bible is full of knowledge and the clergy man preaches it. But none preaches it this way.

V: In the west, Sages did not enjoy freedom to tell the Truth.

M: When I talk here, I have to suffer its effects. That is an established truth.

V: Can you make it more clear.

(Silence.)

Interpreter : Maharaj used to say that *Jnani*'s words are very powerful. They have a great impact on the listeners, including the *Jnani* Himself.

He mentioned about a place of pilgrimage, where a *Jnani* lived long ago. All visitors experienced the secret of that place that they had to leave the place within a few minutes of stay there. Maharaj said any wish of the *Jnani* e.g. "Leave me alone", works even after His *Maha Samadhi*".

A *Jnani* has to be very careful while using words. They have their effect, good or bad, as applicable.

Maharaj did not like burning of crackers due to their sound and air pollution. Once He said, "I wonder why these people burn money and houses." He immediately corrected Himself by saying, "Of course, houses did not get burnt."

M: Prior to His birth, was Jesus aware of appearing in form? It cannot be. He cannot be an exception to the rule.

V: Is there any witness to your Ultimate findings?

M: If there is any witness, be sure it is all a lie. As long as there is no witness, it is all in perfect order and the Truth. In the Absolute state there are no others. I am the only witness of myself.

V: Is Guru's help a must for losing body identity?

M: Yes. Thereafter the disciple gets closer to the Guru.

M: (To a new visitor with closed eyes): Don't meditate here.

Listen with eyes open. When you are alone, go to the state when your parents did not recognise you and you did not recognise them, and meditate deeply.

Do you understand that your appearance in a form was spontaneous?

V: Yes. It was without my knowledge and co-operation.

M: Although you (body) had no knowledge, you the unmanifest Self is responsible for your bodily manifestation.

December 21, 1979

How To Be Free From The 'I Am' Disease?

Maharaj: There is manifestation due to the quintessence of food. The body is born, with the appearance of the three states of waking, sleep and knowingness.

Visitor: Is there anything beyond knowing "I am not this body"?

M: Thereafter, you come to know that you are also not waking, sleep and knowingness. Also, you come to know that you have no birth and you are That which has no beginning and no end.

Your parents were responsible for the body, in which, the news 'you are' appeared. Each of the parents contributed for the appearance of the news. From milk you get butter and ghee. Both these are dormant in milk. Similarly, consciousness is dormant in food. Hence, food sustains consciousness in your body. Your attention (Godess Laxmi) serves your consciousness (God Vishnu)

V: In the picture of God Shiva, river Ganges is shown flowing from His head.

M: Then how could He sleep? Shiva is a great Guru and every utterance of His is profound knowledge. The Ganges is not a flow of water, but of knowledge.

V: Why is God Brahma shown with four mouths?

M: To indicate the four types of speeches: *Para, Pashyanti, Madhyama* and *Vaikhari.*

V: All are speechless here.

M: Outwardly you appear to be silent, but inside the flow of thoughts goes on. Does anyone experience a thought-free state?

(No reply.)

M: In this world we experience so many things. Does any experience remain permanently with us?

V: No.

M: When your vital breath and mind leave and the body drops, what will you be? You love to exist. What will happen to it? Without body-mind how will you look like?

M: Will there be any experience of day and night? What would be your concern about all your close relatives and about your hard earned money and possessions?

(Silence)

M: Who are the parents of all that you see now?

V: Consciousness.

M: 'Without consciousness everything is useless'. Knowing this, will you continue your struggle for more and more?

V: Should we take care to continue consciousness?

M: But it is the quality of a (healthy) food body. Soon consciousness will lose its dwelling place. While it lasts, try to find out what were you without consciousness and how did it make its sudden appearance.

V: That is the best use of consciousness.

M: If I cannot survive without water, it becomes my *Atma* (Self). If consciousness is not , 'I Am' not. Then, consciousness becomes my Self and it should be more important to me than God.

V: All this applies to the ignorant, as well as, to a *Jnani.*

M: The ignorant identifies with the body but a *Jnani* knows that he is neither the body nor the consciousness. He makes use of the consciousness as long as it lasts. He is prior to consciousness and is always in that state.

V: What should a seeker find out?

M (In English): 'I' why, 'I' why?

V: It is a miracle to see the world in a drop of food essence.

M: Every drop or grain of food essence helps to sustain consciousness. You experience the world because of consciousness. Hence, the miracle happens. Hence, we can say that *Sattva* is the father-mother of the whole world. The world is reported to be very ancient, but its parents are drops of fresh juices. It is as if a rubber snake has bitten and there is no end to the effects of poisoning.

V: The world is in consciousness. Hence, the knower of consciousness, who is in the world, should also be in the consciousness.

M: The knower of consciousness is not in consciousness. The consciousness cannot know its knower, the Absolute. An astronomer makes use of a telescope to observe planets and stars. The observer is separate from the telescope, so that he can also observe the telescope. Similarly, the Absolute makes use of the consciousness and It is not in consciousness. The witnessing of consciousness happens to the Absolute and the content is like the content of a TV screen. The Absolute cannot be viewed there. It is always the viewer.

How will you define a poor person?

V: One who has less or no possessions.

M: I decide poverty by the number of desires. The rich have more desires. We cannot expect much from the rich, as they are poor givers. All the moves of the rich, including donations, are directed towards earning more and more.

V: As long as there is consciousness, there are expectations.

M (in English): I want. I want.

V: How to end all wants?

M: You must know the origin of consciousness. Then, one who demands or expects, vanishes.

V: How do you say there is no birth, when there is a specific time and date of birth?

M: It is the birth of time and not of the infant. Time is born not the baby. In your True state you had no knowledge of time. The time started and it will have an end. You are the timeless to whom the time appeared for a certain duration. You are independent of day, night and seasons. What depends on these is the flowing, the transient. You are the witness of all appearances. You imagine yourself to be a somebody in the world that appears to you. Hence, you experience pain and fear. Your unhappiness is the outcome of your own making.

V: How does our knowledge differ from Self-knowledge?

M: The real knowledge is to know the Self. Yours is material knowledge. Your knowing arises due to the material called food juices. What you know is only in the field of the five elements, which is also material. You know only about the family affairs of the five elements, which is time-bound. My knowledge is different from it. I do not depend upon your knowledge. I am timeless. I had no experience of day and night and I was complete and perfect. Your day begins with expectations. How can you be complete?

V: How to be free of the trouble 'I Am'?

M: Sometimes, in our villages, children suddenly develop itching and vomiting sensation, for no apparent reason. The experienced advice to remove the child's shirt. On the skin they notice an insect which normally troubles the cattle. When the insect is removed, the itching and vomiting stops. Similarly, you have to find out the cause of your 'I Am', so that you can be comfortable without it. Your ignorance about the origin of your consciousness is responsible for all your trouble. The thief named 'I amness' vanishes when noticed.

Have you noticed from where your seeing, tasting etc. happens?

V: From brain.

M: It happens from the *Sahasrar Chakra* in the centre of the head.

V: How are the vital breath and the consciousness related?

M: In the food essence, the sense of being is dormant, as if asleep. With the appearance of the pulsation, due to the vital breath, the sense of being or the consciousness takes care to get the food supplies.

V: The name and form help to identify a person.

M: But the body is not one's image. The self-love is one's image. The question of living has arisen due to the appearance of your consciousness. Hence, worship your consciousness as God. Be one with it. Thereby, you will get the required spiritual knowledge and you will be free from unhappiness. The entire knowledge of consciousness unfolds to such a devotee.

V: What is his ultimate achievement?

M: It is the conviction of the Self.

V: Will he be useful to other seekers?

M: He will give them knowledge and help as per their need and worthiness.

Those who are not earnest are satisfied with their verbal knowledge. They become gurus.

V: Many seekers do not stick to one Guru.

M: A seeker left me after visiting me for a number of days. He was not much impressed as I was easily approachable. He expected to get more profound knowledge from some remote cave in the Himalayas. He was surprised to hear the same knowledge from some advanced seeker in the Himalyas. He came back not to leave again. It is not the place that is important, but what is He, who expounds. The Real Guru points out the most important thing which is within the disciple and not outside. When you know 'you are', all other things become important to you. When 'you are' not, what is of importance to you? Instead of wasting your time and energy searching outside, why not sit comfortably and search within?

V: The simple and easy is always unbelievable.

M: Some believe that Self-realization is at the end of a great suffering and sorrow. For them, the Kohinoor diamond cannot be found while walking on a road. They believe that all great things demand great effort to get them.

V: With Self-knowledge our life will become meaningful.

M: When the Self, which is beyond all emotions and consciousness, is realized, all things lose their meaning and importance.

❧

December 22, 1979
You Are The Proof That God Exists

Visitor: Although we hear from you again and again that we are not the bodies, we cannot help taking every care to keep them safe and healthy.

Maharaj: A Sage does not expect anything from the body. He leaves it to nature to do the needful.

V: Does He have any duties to perform?

M: He has no name and form, hence no duties. He is timeless; but the time begins with consciousness. You also experience day and night because of consciousness. With the end of the last day, the consciousness also will be no more. When there is no consciousness, there is no happiness or unhappiness.

What happens to the water in the wet cloth which is left to dry. Similarly, our sense of being is the quality of wet food juices. When the juices get dried up, the sense of being vanishes like water in wet cloth.

V: Were there seekers of Truth in the past?

M: Princes like Mahaveer and Buddha left their kingdoms in search of Truth. For them Self-knowledge was more important than the comforts of ignorance.

V: How is the company of a Sage, useful?

M: One comes to know the importance of *vairagya* (detachment). Its practice helps in understanding the Sadguru. When I visited my hometown recently after a long gap, there was none there to recognise me. All my acquaintances were dead earlier. Similarly, what I was acquainted with myself as "so and so", that acquaintance has also gone. That knower of acquaintance also is no more. My state is beyond all acquaintance and recognition. In this process of knowing, there was an indication that I was born. But that was seen as untrue. Just as all our identities from an infant to an old man, change with time, all my knowledge about myself got erased and lost. It did not concern me at all. Even the sign of birth was recognised, but it became clear that it also did not concern me. Just as in my home town I do not own anything, this birth was also not my own.

M: *(To a new visitor)*: A hundred years ago your knowingness was absent. Now, it is present. Why?

V: Due to my birth.

M: Your knowingness was absent at your birth. Otherwise, you would have remembered it. The knowingness appeared 3 to 5 years after the birth of the body. Are you responsible for your birth?

V: No. It happened without my knowledge.

M: Two people had some enjoyment and a third had to suffer for no reason. Eighty two years back a young couple had a nice time together and I have been suffering all these 82 years. Once you know that it is not your birth and that you have nothing to do with it, you are free.

V: Are we responsible for our thoughts?

M: As long as there is breathing, the thought-flow goes on. You make use of some thought and ignore others. Why should you be responsible? But do not get involved with thoughts. Remain free.

How is your existence related to that of God's?

V: God is great; hence 'I Am'.

M: Because God is, you are there. But you are the proof that God exists. Your's and God's existence is mutually interdependent. Your existence is because of your parents. Now, your parents exist in your form. You prove the existence of your parents. Are you a real seeker?

V: Yes.

M: A real seeker loves to be in the Company of a Sage. He listens to Him with great attention. The Sage makes him bodiless. That is real thread ceremony. *Brahmins* start wearing a thread after that ceremony.

A *mumukshu* is one who desires liberation. When he learns that he is not the body, he becomes a seeker, a *Sadhaka*. The name is given to the body. Hence, the bodiless (*Videhi*) becomes nameless. One's true nature without name and form is to be realized. On what does existence depend?

V: On God.

M: Its is nameless. Let us call It *Paramatma*, so as to understand what I mean. It is wordless, timeless and even without consciousness. Just as the earth supports all life on it, the entire existence is because of *Paramatma*. The existence of *Paramatma* is as if non-existence. Still It is Eternal. All other existence appears so much and so true; but it is all time-bound. The time bound can be known, but not the Eternal, which is always the knower and not the known.

V: That was our being a hundred years ago.

M: Yes. It cannot be known in duality; but you are It, in non-duality. People want the joy of knowing It, which is not possible. In that sense, It is unworldly.

All that is time-bound, including great incarnations, is untrue. Only the Eternal is the Truth. All Gods with name and form are not Eternal.

V: All names and forms have a beginning and hence, an end.

M: Can the waking state talk to the deep sleep state?

V: No.

M: One side of a coin cannot see the other. Nothing gets finished. The small vanishes to become big. A water drop evaporates to become an ocean. The stocks of food grains go on increasing year after year. There is consciousness in various forms and we have a man, a horse or a donkey. Because of consciousness there is a sense of being. This sense of being when gone, is not available again.

V: What is responsible for this light of consciousness?

M: It is due to burning of the food essence (*Sattva*) in the body. You are sitting here and you know it without effort. Before that, the Principle which is without consciousness, knows it. Thereafter you come to know it, and your me and mine begin.

In the morning that Principle, which is without consciousness, knows that there is waking. Thereafter, the body identity begins with the me and mine. Then the worldly activities begin.

The Marathi word for waking is *Jagrati*. This word can be split into *Jag* (waking) + *Rati*. *Rati* means small and also it means the joy of union of the male and female. Thus, our

166

waking state is the result of the short sexual enjoyment of our parents. Our worldly life is the operation of that waking state. If you meditate on this, you will know the secret of the consciousness and your separation from it.

M: I am making these secrets so clear and open for you; but you lack the capacity to grasp it and be free. *Brahman* is very ancient, which has two aspects, which are also ancient. One is *Prakriti* and the other is *Purusha*. Both are formless; but without them, no forms are possible. Both are responsible for all creation, including that of the smallest sprout. These deserve your attention more than *Vaikuntha* and *Kailas*, the hearsay abodes of God Vishnu and Shiva.

V: Everybody knows that our parents were responsible for our arrival. We do not know its spiritual significance.

M: Meditation on your parents' conjugal bliss will show you how it is the birth of an illusion and not you. You, the Eternal, did not know 'you are'. Thereafter the Eternal started knowing that It existed. The ever existing started knowing Its existence. The bliss enjoyed by parents was formless and the news 'I Am' which was also formless, appeared in a form i.e. the physical body. You are the presence mark of your parents.

Your consciousness is the result of the bliss enjoyed by your parents. Hence, the term *Chidananda* (*chit*, to perceive + *ananda*, joy) i.e. consciousness-bliss. Its importance is enhanced by adding Sat i.e. *Satchidananda* (existence-consciousness-bliss).

M: All living forms have consciousness resulting from the consciousness-bliss of their parents. Your consciousness is a suffering resulting from that bliss. Your consciousness contains your world. Hence, your world is the result of that consciousness-bliss of your parents. The parents are not individuals but the formless *Prakriti* and *Purusha*. Many learned people would get wonder-struck by my simple Marathi words.

V: Their content is so profound and awakening.

M: What is it that entered the womb and was responsible for the growth?

V: Chidananda (consciousness-bliss)

M: Did that bliss have any form? No. Then what happened ? Meditate on it.

That consciousness-bliss became the content of a womb and it turned into "I love" of somebody, in due course.

❧

December 23, 1979

YOUR PARENTS ARE GOLD, AND YOU THE ORNAMENT
ঞ্চ

Maharaj : All your knowledge is a hearsay. What do you really know, other than that?

Visitor: We also learn from experiences.

M: You are prior to all experiences and you have to learn your Self. Do you understand that you are experiencing the world without any effort?

V: Yes. It is spontaneous.

M: You have to go to the root and have conviction about your true nature. Your understanding, which changes with time, is untrue. The changeless is true.

When you know 'you are', your worldly activities begin. But prior to knowing 'you are' what are you? Be there. Your true state is without the knowledge 'you are'. Having stabilized in the state prior to consciousness Sage Tukaram said, "Now, God is taking care of all my activities. I was not able to express properly. He has given it clarity. I was shy and timid. He has made me bold."

V: What is the origin of this world?

M: From the no-knowing (*Ajnana*) state appears the 'I Am' knowledge (*Jnana*), in which there is your world. The *ajnana* state continues from womb to over three years of your age. This applies to all world heroes and even to incarnations like Ram and Krishna. The birth of knowledge (consciousness) is in ignorance.

V: The term ignorance (*ajnana*) is disturbing.

M: Then you can call it *Vijnana* – That which is prior to knowledge or beyond knowledge (*jnana*).

M (to a visitor): The memory 'you are', is it not the memory that your parents were?

V: Yes.

M: It is like a golden ornament. You are the ornament; but the parents are gold.

V: How to recognize a *Jnani*?

M: He does not have any ego. Even the feeling that I am a *Jnani* and different from others, is absent.

V: I have gained a lot by coming here.

M: But you have lost your birth itself. You can go anywhere, but the knower of Self is very rare to find. You will come across great scholars, speakers and Mahatmas. But they are of no use to the real seekers. When you arrive at your True identity, you are wonderstruck to find our, "Am I really nothing?"

V: The four Vedas expound Self-knowledge.

M: With folded hands they have accepted their inability to expound Truth. The Truth has no colour, no form. It is beyond words. No religious practices can take you to the Eternal Truth.

Although the worldly existence is a meaningless suffering,

the ignorant have no option. A disciple of a Sage tried hard for Self-realization, without success. On his last day he said, "I trust my Guru that I am *Brahman*, whole and complete" and left his mortal coil.

M (to visitor): Are you really free to live as you like and avoid suffering?

V: The wise can minimise suffering. They cannot avoid it.

M: Even this form has been forced on me. It has been changing throughout my life. Try to find out your most humble unchanging identity. In this existence, everything is changing so fast that stability is only imaginary or a wishful thinking. Dishonesty is the rule. Even if you imagine changeless conditions, you are yourself not changeless to enjoy them. The creation of vegetation during a rainy season is short lived. We are also a result of a shower (of sperms). I remember some lines of *Dasbodh*:

> *All that appeared to exist, vanished.*
> *What did not exist, was not.*
> *What remained after the above two,*
> *The indiscribable, It exited as if non-existent,*
> *Paramatma alone exists as nothing;*
> *but it is at the root of everything.*
> *"I AM THAT"*

V: I do not know what I am.

M: This bodily existence is like an accident.

Prior to this accident, say a hundred years back, you have direct knowledge of that state.

V: After Self-knowledge what remains to be done?

M: Nothing. No duties remain.

V: Buddha said be your own light.

M: If you don't have your own light, you have to take help of others' light. Due to ignorance, you consult others. When you have your own light, others come to you. There is no repentance about the past and no worries about the future. His state is described as *Sahajawastha* – the most natural and spontaneous state. I look like others, but my illusion has gone. Hence, there are no expectations.

V: Why is knowledge 'I Am' (consciousness) so important?

M: It is the soul of your world – no 'I Am', no world. The root of consciousness is a moment, or to be precise, only a fraction of a moment. Of what is this moment, you have to find out. One who knows that moment, sees oneself as unborn.

When you wake up in the morning, for a very short duration, there is pure being without words. Try to watch it, before your thoughts disturb it. The same pure state existed upto three years or so after the birth of the body. It lasted until you recognised your mother.

I give you useful hints and try to awaken you. I respect the visitors for all their interest. But they find it difficult to understand me.

V: Who gets the news 'I Am'?

M: Of course, it is the unborn who gets it. Before that it did not have the news. Because of this news it appears that the unborn has got bound by the chain of birth. One who knows the secret of this news, knows the moment of the root of consciousness. Then one sees oneself as unborn and free. Your conviction of birth itself is the bondage.

V: Our true nature is without attributes. It is almost a non-entity.

M: The existence is great, but it is dream like. There was conception due to the conjugal bliss. The consciousness-bliss entered the womb and grew in the foetus. The foetus had a form but not the consciousness-bliss. It was the growth of the 'I love' in dormant condition.

V: Should we stabilize prior to 'I love'.

M: Just meditate on 'I love'.

V: A pregnant woman takes so much care of herself.

M: It is the consciousness, which is responsible for all the protection and also of the foetus. The world that I experience is on my own. It is not anybody's favour to me.

V: It is said *Brahman* is real and world is false.

M: There is this world and we have its knowledge. Both these, as well as, *Ishwara* (God) are false. I know it. Still my talk goes on.

V: As *Parabrahman*, what is your experience?

M: The experience of the individual soul, the world and *Brahman* was absent. Its experience, now, is like having a fever. As every child is an appearance of the Absolute in a form, it has to begin the worldly experience with no-knowledge. In the Absolute there was nothing. Now, the child finds many different new things and beings around it. Hence, the never ending questions of every child, which are but natural. The child may be only a few days or months old; but there is the Eternal.

V: I met a Sadhu who claimed to have the knowledge of *Brahman*. The Self-knowledge was of no importance to him.

M: If he comes to me, I will ask him, a hundred years back you had no problems. They are there, now. Why and how? Until you find it out, your misery will remain intact despite your so-called knowledge of *Brahman*. Some people become

Gurus by having a few visions of Gods. Illusions cannot lead one to Truth.

V: What is the importance of spontaneity?

M: All your actions should be smooth and effortless. You cannot put in effort to go to sleep. If you do, you remain awake.

With Self-knowledge, the ego dissolves. Life becomes spontaneous.

December 24, 1979

WHAT IS *SAHAJA* YOGA?

Maharaj: All creation is because of the five elements. Is there any profit or loss for these elements? Only human beings have that idea.

Visitor: What about other living beings?

M: In the absence of intelligence, there is no question of any profit and loss. Activities of the five elements go on without any control.

V: Man has made so much development in this world.

M: He takes pleasure in developing even the imaginary abodes of Vishnu (*Vaikuntha*) and Shiva (*Kailas*). All man made things are short lived. What has a beginning must also have an end. Only the Self is changeless. To realize It, you must meditate on consciousness i.e. remain in a thought-free state, as long as possible. With realization you will come to know that this experience of the world that you are having, is all useless. You will come to know that your world is in your mind. To know it, you must be free of all involvement. Otherwise, you cannot accept reality and you prefer to be in your imagination. With realization your 'I Am' vanishes and what remains is your true Self.

V: What is unreal?

M: You consider yourself to be that, which you are not. Acceptance of the unreal is your trouble and it will last until the True is realized. Do not blame anybody for dishonesty. What changes every moment cannot be honest. In this, everything is changing, including your own identity.

V: Do you also have worries?

M: Here, what is there to worry? From your own experience, can you say that there is nobody to worry?

V: No. I am scared of death. What about a *Jnani*?

M: Suppose a patient has a urinary problem and there is no urination for three days. If the problem is solved and there is normal urination, how will he feel? A *Jnani* has the same joy when the vital breath leaves the body and the consciousness becomes no-conscious. It is described as *Paramananda*.

V: Self-realization seems to be the only solution to all problems.

M: I was accused of having been born, and I was suffering. But my Guru showed me that I was never born. I was That which always exists and cannot be born. Hence, my suffering ended.

V: What is *Sahaja Yoga* (easy natural yoga).

M: It is to meditate on your consciousness as God. You need not go anywhere for it. Do it wherever you are. There is no equipment required to do it. No outer help required. Be with yourself.

V: How to meditate?

M: Knowing that you are not your body, hold your consciousness with itself.

V: We should not just imagine as we are told, but actually be it.

M: When you woke up in the morning, who came to know it?

V: It takes some time to know that I am really awake.

M: All these talks are really to wake you up. A hundred years back you had no experience of day and night, waking and sleep, and also of conscious and non-conscious. That is timeless experience. The present one is time-bound.

V: Sri Ramana Maharshi and Sri Anandamayi Ma were asked whether they sleep. They said 'No'. Does a *Jnani* have any attraction to existence in a form?

M: No. Everyone sees the dream of birth in which One is born and in the same dream sees one's parents. Birth is the happening of the bliss of sexual union, along with the appearance of the dormant memory 'I Am'. Birth is the transition from no 'I Am' state to 'I Am' state.

V: How can I be complete, total and perfect?

M: You are already That from which your 'I Am' knowledge and the experience of day and night have arisen. Only your ignorance has to drop. The experience is termed as the world. Do not get over impressed by great things. It is really the greatness of your vision that is imparted to those things. Your vision is the primary illusion or the great God.

V: What is Guru's job?

M: The knowledge about my Self was available with me earlier. My Guru only reminded me about it. Everything is my expression and all will merge into me finally.

V: How do you differ from time?

M: Time has a beginning and an end. I have none.

V: How do I differ from my sense of being?

M: The sense of being is the quality of the three *gunas* (qualities) of *Sattva*, *Rajas* and *Tamas*. You are not these qualities and are separate from them.

V: Can I know my Self by reading scriptures?

M: Do you know 'you are' by reading books?

V: Some times I have a feeling that I know my Self.

M: As long as that feeling is there, be sure that the freedom and joy of Self-realization is not there. Until the concept of birth is there, one is not out of ignorance.

V: Why am I not yet free?

M: You are trying to remind yourself to be the Self; but your body identity is intact. Before saying 'I Am' what you are, is your true Self.

V: What is my difficulty?

M: It is easy to make use of consciousness, but it is difficult to get established as consciousness. The body identity remains in the background. You see with your eyes but do not see the eyes. While making use of consciousness, you should also be aware of consciousness. The use of consciousness does not give you peace and tranquility. That is possible only by establishing as consciousness.

V: What is the reason for our fear and unhappiness?

M: If you are a painter and you work as a dentist, there will be fear and unhappiness. Similarly, you have accepted the work of the three *gunas* (qualities) as your own work. Hence, all these problems trouble you.

V: What are we, if not these bodies?

M: You are neither the bodies nor the consciousness. In the body there is the news 'you are'. How can you be your news? You are separate from it. You give different names to living food bodies of different sizes and shapes like man, horse, donkey etc. There is use of photography to create bodies of the same types.

V: If we are the Reality, why follow any religious practices?

M: The ignorant follow them for the satisfaction of following a tradition and also for entertainment.

V: Our existence is almost like a dream.

M: Our consciousness is like the light of an oil lamp, which burns as long as there is oil. When there is nothing to burn, the light gets extinguished. There is no coming or going. No heaven, no hell.

December 25, 1979

I Am In A
No-Knowledge State

Ꙩ

Visitor: Is there any choice in life?

Maharaj: The consciousness comes unknowingly and one is forced to live with it. Self knowledge helps to minimise suffering and then be free of it.

V: My body is my bondage.

M: If you are not the body, how will it bind you? There is neither bondage nor unhappiness for you.

V: Am I *Atma* (Self)?

M: Yes. You had the company of J. Krishnamurti. How are you still ignorant?

V: When I wake up in the morning, for a short time I am not my body.

M: You, the nameless and formless, first witness the consciousness and then other things including the body. Then, you act taking yourself as the body.

V: What is the difference between a *Jnani* and an infant?

M: In a *Jnani* there is an end of all knowledge and in an infant, it is yet to begin.

V: What is *Shaktipat?*

M: I understand it as weakness after meditation or a feeling of lightness. I do not know what others mean by that term.

V: Is the loss of body identity, Self-realization?

M: It is only the beginning of Self-realization.

V: What applies to you, should it also apply to me?

M: We are one. There is no difference. The Principle which is in you, is talking to you, through me. You have forgotten yourself. But I, who is in you, have not forgotten you. Just as I love myself, I love you equally. When you realize yourself, all scriptures will flow out of you and you will simply listen. Without Self-knowledge whatever you have collected in this world, who will be its master after you? Because 'you are' you bother about others. When you 'were not' what was your botheration? Is it not of the utmost importance to find out the cause of 'I Am' from the eternal state of "No-I Am"? God Ganapati's second name is Vinayak. I call it as *Vina yeka* i.e. without one. With the counting of one, the further counting of two, three etc. upto infinity goes on. *Vinayak* is prior to one, in the non-dual Absolute.

Our breathing in and out creates sounds. One sound appears to be a question about our identity followed by a sound which gives the reply. Let us see how? Breathing in produces sound *ko* (who) *ham* (am I?). The next breath out replies *So* (That) *ham* (I Am). This question-answer about our identity goes on continuously all the twenty four hours and a seeker has only to give attention to it.

V: You seem to have a good stock of knowledge.

M: No. I am in a no-knowledge state. To every question the reply comes from the *Nirvikalpa* (thought free state) and the witnessing happens to me. I am here to help you get rid of your hard earned stocks.

V: Is it possible to mistake one's own self as Self-realized?

M: Quite so. That is what we notice all around us. More than cheating others, these Gurus are cheating themselves. Their most fond concept is that they are free of all concepts. Every Guru has a big following, and the relation between disciples of different Gurus is far from friendly. They avoid even facing one another.

One who has pure Self knowledge is a true Guru.

The Eternal is the Truth and it is open to all. A true Guru cannot produce a witness, as there are no others in that state.

V: There is only peace and tranquility in the company of a Sage.

M: What you are in reality is so peaceful that it does not need anything to pacify it. What you are not i.e. body, mind and consciousness, is so disturbing that it cannot be pacified by any actions. All worldly activities are meant to be comfortable in the mistaken identity.

V: People are carrying on with their religious practices and even idol worship.

M: The idol cannot protect itself. It is covered with crow's droppings. The offerings made by people is eaten by rats. With all this background the idol is believed to be very powerful and a giver of all that is desired. This faith itself works wonders.

V: How do people see visions of Gods of their liking?

M: Consciousness is like the Kohinoor diamond. You see visions of Vishnu, Shiva, Hanuman, Ganapati or even of ghosts, if you choose.

December 26, 1979

My Guru Is *Parabrahman*

Maharaj: Because of your consciousness you know everything, but you do not know why and how this consciousness has appeared. It is necessary to know that.

Visitor: Is my *Atma* (Self) responsible for my wrong doings?

M: Whatever you do with your body identity, your *Atma* is not responsible for it. *Atma* is only a witness.

V: What about meditation with body identity?

M: It will never give you peace and tranquility.

V: You never advise us about worldly activities.

M: I take you to the source. Once you know It, your activities will be in order. Any type of activities cannot lead to knowledge.

V: What is the use of mind?

M: Your thought flow is your mind. It is disturbing in spirituality. It should be under control, just as you control an animal by pulling the string passing through its nostrils.

V: How do ideas turn into reality?

M: Your attention is drawn to the idea that occurs to you.

You were in Antwerp (Belgium) and now you are here in Bombay (Mumbai). How? Because idea of visiting Bombay occurred to you after reading "I AM THAT". If you had not read that book, you would have been in Antwerp only. King Shah Jahan thought of a beautiful memorial for his dead wife Mumtaj Mahal; and there was the construction of Taj Mahal at Agra.

V: Some Gurus have a spiritual profession.

M: But my Guru is *Parabrahman* and I have full faith in Him.

I am prior to all concepts. Hence, they do not affect me. Just as you are undisturbed by clouds moving in the sky, I watch the thoughts which appear occassionally.

M: Paramatma does not seem to be interested in publicity.

M: The 'I Am' knowledge is His advertisement. The various incarnations are His publicity.

V: Without consciousness we are *Paramatma*. After committing suicide are we *Paramatma*?

M: No. The suicide is a deliberate action. The transition should be spontaneous.

V: If one has glimpses of one's true nature, is it realization?

M: One must have conviction of one's true nature. In the true Eternal state, one cannot find a witness to one's true condition. Also, one does not need it. As long as there is need to prove one's realization, there is no realization. The false can be proved as true, by false methods.

In the True state one loses all attributes. In the Eternal non-conscious attributeless state the appearance of 'I Am' is for so short a duration relatively, as if it never appeared at all.

A *Jnani* is never bothered about all existence as it is as good as false. Any way, it does not affect the Eternal.

V: Is egg first or the hen?

M: The news 'you are' is the egg of your world, Here, the egg comes first and then the hen. I am separate from the news and unaffected by the world.

Where did you get the memory you are from?

V: In my mother's womb.

M: What was not there and which appeared subsequently?

V: The news 'I Am'.

December 27, 1979

WHAT IS *BODHISATTVA*?

Maharaj: There is the vast tree above the ground because of the underground roots. Where is your world, if your 'I Am' knowledge is absent? Your world is the light of your Self (Atmaprakash).

Visitor: What is implied meaning of the following Marathi verse:

"The infant Hari urinated in the cradle, as if a stone pricked Him."

M: All living forms including human beings are expressions of God Hari. Our sense of being is like a prick of a stone. To forget it we go on doing something or the other. Here the shower is not of urine, but of sperms. It is said that there is misery in this world. But its population is ever increasing year by year.

V: Where do all these people go finally?

M: Suppose there is a big fire. Where does it go finally?

V: Nowhere.

M: It merges into itself. Similarly, we have appeared from the non-being state, into which we finally merge. When we are tired we go to sleep; but the no-being state is even prior to sleep.

The manifestation has rising and setting. The rising is called waking and the setting is called sleep. The no-being state has no rising and setting.

All that exists is we only and all that vanishes is also we.

V: Why don't we make progress faster?

M: If you wish to ask any questions, keep aside your body identity and talk. With your body identity intact, none of your problems will get solved. A person went in search of darkness, with a torch in hand. He could not find darkness anywhere. Similarly, it is not possible for the manifest to search for the unmanifest. There is the unmanifest only in the absence of the manifest.

V: What should I know?

M: You must have complete knowledge of your consciousness, just as you can clearly see a berry on your palm.

V: What is my main obstacle?

M: Your body identity. Not even the slightest of it is permissible. One who dwells in one's identity without the body, makes progress.

V: Different seekers have different problems.

M: Although the consciousness is one and the same, its expression changes from form (person) to form. Ten children of the same mother may have ten qualities. The expression is mischievous.

V: Is a *Jnani* full of knowledge?

M: There is no knowledge but pure being. A mountain of attributes appear on the attributeless Eternal state.

V: Why are people after enjoyment?

M: The sense of being is miserable. In order to forget it one seeks enjoyment or any occupation. Our 'I am-ness' is like a scorpion bite. One has to do something in order to tolerate it or forget it. You call it work or enjoyment. In deep sleep you had no problems. A hundred years back also you had no problems. It is because there was no 'I am-ness'.

V: Are you an incarnation of God?

M: No. I am like you. All human beings are equal and have the ability to know themselves, but a rare one uses the ability and becomes free.

V: Is there any remedy to inherited defects?

M: The defects in the food juices called parents are passed on to the next generation. Yoga i.e. *yogic* postures (*asanas*) and *pranayam* is the remedy. It is the best preventive and also a cure.

The Marathi word for seed is *beeja*. It is also means copying, like photocopying. Hence, the identical nature or similarity of the offshoots.

God Hari is a manifestation of the Absolute. He is wearing a *dhoti* the colour of which is the mixture of yellow and white. In Marathi we call it *Peetambara*, i.e. yellow+white. Yellow is the colour of *Prakriti* and white that of *Purusha* (Panduranga).

V: How do you say that there is no birth?

M: I know that there was a time when our sense of being was absent. Its appearance is birth according to me. In the Absolute, that is the only extra-ordinary happening. All living beings have to act as per the thoughts or inspiration that flows from within.

What is the most fundamental thing with every human being?

V: The 'I Am' feeling or thought.

M: Other thoughts and actions follow this fundamental thought. When there was no sense of being was there any unhappiness? Was there any need for happiness?

V: No.

M: There is a story of a successful man. He earned billions, helped thousands and became world famous. What was at the root of all his success? It was his sense of being. Without it he could not have done anything. Hence, your sense of being is the most important thing with you. Give attention to it. Meditate on it and it will tell you all its, i.e. your, secrets. That is the knowledge of the Self or Self-realization. With the sense of being there is our world and our concept that there is God. Hence, at the centre of all is our 'I Am'.

V: You never visit any Sages or Mahatmas.

M: All our knowledge and its content, including Sages and Mahatmas, depend upon the 'I Am' knowledge, which is time-bound and false. Hence, I do not visit anybody.

V: Yesterday, you said you do not wish to impart this knowledge to anybody, why?

M: When I investigated this knowledge 'I Am', it turned against me, liquidating all my beliefs. Why should I irritate others with that knowledge? People are quite comfortable as they are, without this knowledge. What will you do in a state, where there is neither remembering nor forgetting?

V: But our present state does not give us peace and happiness.

M: That is also true. All your knowledge is based on the 'I Am' knowledge, which has appeared spontaneously. You do not know the why and how of it. But for peace and happiness, that knowledge is a must.

V: A man may be very great and famous; but all his greatness depends upon the news 'I Am' which has appeared spontaneously and which can leave any moment. When it goes, where is his greatness?

M: Happiness and peace is possible only after the secret of 'I Am' is known. Then, it does not remain just a news; but it attains Godhood.

V: What do these people who do daily *bhajans* and visit God Vithoba of Pandharpura regularly, gain thereby?

M: These people are immersed in *bhajans* and Vithoba. They see Him even in dreams and in visions. This helps them to forget all worries and be fearless on the day of passing. The vital breath of these devotees leaves in a great joy. From their last day you can judge how they must have lived throughout their lives.

For other people even a thought of death is dreadful. They see messengers of God Yama and die a miserable death.

There is no heaven or hell. It only matters how you die, whether merrily or in fear. You begin construction of any building laying a stone. What do you call it.?

V: Foundation stone.

M: Your knowledge 'I Am' is the foundation of your universe. 'I Am' are the feet of the God of Universe (*Vishwambhara*). Meditate on that 'I Am' without words, in order to propitiate it. It will tell you all its (i.e. yours) secrets. It will become clear to you that you are neither the body nor the mind. There will be a transformation in you. Your thought flow will continue, but with less number and of a higher quality. They will be thoughts of *Brahman*. Your needs will be less and they will be met spontaneously, without effort. The activities of the body, mind and the vital breath will continue, but you will only remain their witness.

V: How will I see my death?

M: The departure of the vital breath and mind will be witnessed by you. You will see the body inert on the bed and the consciousness becoming non-conscious. It is like witnessing the passing of urine or stools. The observers will say you are dead, but it will not be your experience.

I welcome profound questions. Do you have any?

(Silence)

M: You know 'you are' (*Swavishaya*) and everything is contained in it. What else do you know?

V: That itself is everything.

M: When you are everything, you cannot have any problems. Your greatest blunder is your identification with the body. Your body identity is incomplete. When you know it and it goes, you are already complete.

V: What is so unique about our consciousness?

M: The Sun is great but cannot see darkness. Also, the darkness cannot see the Sun. But you (consciousness) can see both these. That is your greatness.

V: We were lucky to be born.

M: A hundred years back you were complete in all respects. The so called birth is of incompleteness.

V: What is *Bodhisattva* (of Buddha)?

M: You have bodha (knowledge) that 'you are' because of *Sattva* body. Hence, you are *Bodhisattva*.

V: Is a long life useful?

M: Somebody lived for two hundred years. What is the use? It is almost like urinating while standing in some remote corner.

December 28, 1979

IS 'DESTINY' A CONCEPT?

Visitor: I have fear of death. Why?

Maharaj: Your body was born and it is going to die. Your fear is due to your identification with the body. You must know what you are. Then you will enjoy the joy of getting rid of pain and fear.

V: How to meditate?

M: I call *Dhyan* (meditation) as *Jnana* (knowledge 'you are'). Can you be without the knowledge 'you are'?

V: No.

M: Hence, meditation goes on in you. It needs only your attention. Take knowledge 'you are' as your Guru and give attention to it, as long as possible. Hold on to your consciousness, which is the seed of Self-knowledge. Thereby, you will know the Self.

V: Why do we suffer so much in life?

M: You are reducing your Guru's greatness to the body level. Hence you suffer.

V: What is *Maya*?

M: That which has no existence is asserting herself as present.

That is *Maya*. *Ma* means not, *ya* means which. That which has no existence is *Maya*.

V: Do you believe in miracles?

M: When I did not know my existence, there was nothing. My existence and the world have appeared simultaneously. Is it not a miracle?

V: Will my world last indefinitely?

M: It will last only as long as your consciousness lasts.

V: How long will I be interested in this world and its objects?

M: As long as your body identity remains.

V: What is the origin of all arts?

M: The intelligence is due to the consciousness in human form. The consciousness is due to *Sattva* or food essence, which is in turn due to the five elements. Hence, all arts are due to the five elements.

V: Do all living beings follow any commandments?

M: They do follow certain rules out of fear and instinct and not to please God.

V: All living bodies are made of five elements.

M: In one respect all bodies are similar.

V: They are food of consciousness.

M: They are also one another's food. No sane God would create such survival system. Hence, all creation is spontaneous.

V: Why are we always in need of something or the other?

M: Because of your individuality. A *Jnani* loses his individuality and is free of desire. His activities happen spontaneously. Sage Jnaneshwar has written about a *Jnani* as, "The whole universe becomes His home or to be more precise, He becomes one with all the movable and the immovable". He becomes one with all the five elements. A *Jnani* knows the world, but the world knows Him only by His miracles.

V: How is the *Jnani* so sure of not being the body?

M: The body is made of the five elements, which the *Jnani* is not. Hence, *Jnani* is not the body. The same applies to all others, who insist that they are the bodies. All existence is time-bound, but the knower of time is timeless. Where there is consciousness there is time. But the knower of Consciousness is timeless; and the timeless cannot be time-bound. The clock of the primary illusion ticks at a very slow rate. When billions of years pass, the clock of *Maya* ticks only a second. It indicates as if nothing ever happened. Do you experience the world in your life or you experience your life in your world?

V: We experience our life in this world.

M: If you are not, where is your world? Hence, you come first and then your world. You experience the world in your life.

V: Don't you experience time now?

M: The time is there for last eighty two years only. But it is very clear what I was eternally, when the time was not. Hence, I talk whatever I want to. It is not my imagination, but what is really so. How can the Eternal be measured by time i.e. from-to. I do not need a witness in support of these facts.

V: But you are making use of consciousness to talk about the non-conscious state.

M: Without consciousness how can I convey? I am not consciousness, but I make use of it when needed. I am the witness of consciousness, which is my instrument.

V: What is *Prarabdha* (destiny)?

M: 'The effects of good and bad deeds of this and past lives get stored in one's account. One has to enjoy or suffer according to one's actions.' This is the normal belief about *Prarabdha*. It is all untrue for me. The main point is, man must get strength from somewhere to face life as it comes and when it comes. When I think of *Prarabdha*, I remember the head-load relieving pillars erected in our villages. Formerly, in Indian Villages there were no cars or buses. The rich had bullock carts and others had to walk short or long distances. Almost every person had light or heavy load of personal belongings like fire wood, purchased goods, produce for sale, luggage etc. This load was normally carried on the head. After travelling long distances one needed relief from the load for taking rest and drink water etc. Keeping this requirement in mind short pillars of human height were erected at various places in rural areas. It was a great relief to the travellers to transfer the load to the top of the pillar and be free for sometime. Thus refreshed they would begin their journey again. The concept of *Prarabdha* helps people in a similar manner. Untimely death of young people is explained as their *Prarabdha*. They were allotted only short lives by God in this life. People used to console themselves saying they had done something bad in the past lives and it was necessary to suffer now to wipe out the evil of past lives. Without such explanation and consolation, life would have become very difficult and even intolerable for many. Hence, the concept of *Prarabdha* serves to provide relief to the ignorant people. Even in these modern times many take help of this old concept to face life as it comes.

V: What is birth?

M: It is the appearance of a tiny ball of the five elements with dormant consciousness. When I know that I cannot be this ball, why should I take it as my birth?

V: What happens when I meditate on my consciousness?

M: You will get knowledge of your true being. The Truth will become crystal clear. 'What is' will open up.

V: That has produced Sages.

M: If I meet a Sage, I will see that ball of the five elements at His root. You have not investigated your own roots. Hence, you are not comfortable with your beingness. For peace and happiness you have to visit a Sage, who tells you what you are and instructs you how to meditate. A Sage is not different from you, but you have to realize the Unity.

V: Where do the words originate?

M: Word is the quality of space. Words originate in the space and they finally land on the earth. They become a part of the vegetation. That is consumed by the various living forms, from whose mouths the words come out. The first words are the sense of being, 'I Am'.

V: Are not our lives limited?

M: The duration of your life is like the duration of the Olympic games. These games have a beginning and an end. At the end, all the participants etc. leave. The witnessing that was happening is not happening now. That's it. Similarly in reality you are the witness of your life. You are the unborn to whom the witnessing happens for a certain duration. The end of the body does not mean death of the witness. Our life is the duration of witnessing.

V: Should one commit suicide in case of a failure?

M: No. The quality of this consciousness is mysterious and unpredictable. It can make one very successful again in no time. In a speck of consciousness there dwells the whole world.

V: If I know the origin of this consciousness, is it enough?

M: Then your work will be done. Then you will see yourself as unborn. You will lose your name and form, and become timeless.

V: Do I die with the body?

M: You are that which separates from the body on death.

V: Am I in the world or the world is in me?

M: You and your world are one.

V: As consciousness, I should always be happy.

M: You are living as the body and becoming unhappy.

V: Do I have freedom to act?

M: You, as the Absolute, are not the doer, but only a witness. Your activities happen because of the God in you. You know that actions like sleeping and excretion happen. You cannot do them.

V: How do 'I love', *Maya* and *Ishwara* differ?

M: They are all one only.

V: Should I tell this knowledge to my relatives and friends?

M: No. It is meant for you only. Meditate on it.

December 29, 1979

YOU ARE TAKEN CARE OF
❧

Maharaj: An astronomer uses a telescope to see distant objects; but he is not the telescope. Similarly, the witness of consciousness and its content is not the consciousness.

Visitor: What is the cause of our fear?

M: The fear is because of your body identity. Only the formless can be fearless.

V: If I am not the body, will I tend to neglect it?

M: I am not this flower pot and the flowers, but I do take care of them. The loss of body identity does not mean neglect of the body. There will be care of the body without any worry or anxiety.

What do you see with closed eyes?

V: Nothing.

M: You see deep blue or deep black. The body functions as long as That can be seen. It is called *Megha Shyam* or dark-complexioned Krishna and also as *Savla Ram* or dark-complexioned Ram.

V: You have told us that we are already perfect before doing anything. The only requirement is proper understanding.

M: At other places you will be asked to do this and that. It is their business. A *Jnani* is the knower of the transition from the no knowing state to the knowing state.

When you wake up from sleep, who comes to know it?

V: The consciousness.

M: With closed eyes you see the deep blue or black. On opening the eyes you see first the space and then the other things. A rare disciple of a Sage declares that he has found his eternal dwelling place. The timeless is beyond being and non-being.

V: Does the world have an independent existence?

M: A Sage sees the world as His beingness.

V: We can meet a Sage who has a body. How to contact Him when He is without a body?

M: He is one and the same as you were a hundred years back. You did exist, but without the knowledge 'you are'. The same state continued even in the womb and thereafter upto over three years of your age.

V: How does the knowledge 'I Am' develop from the no-knowing state?

M: It is like sweetening of a raw mango.

V: How can one plan from the no-knowing state to take birth again?

M: The ignorant say so and the listeners are made to believe it. All your so called knowledge is of that type.

V: If you are the unborn, ever existing Principle, is it not an offence to talk of your birth?

M: It is. It is like accusing me of leading a gang of docoits, which robbed a bank in New Delhi. How can I accept responsibility for that crime? Hence, I reject my birth as an impossibility.

V: Is there perception in non-duality?

M: How can that be? A slightest difference or change is a must to notice. In oneness who will perceive whom? When there is you, there is also I. *Parabrahman* alone exists. It is alone or all one. It does not know its existence or there is no 'I Am' knowledge or beingness in *Parabrahman*. In the complete, there is no experience. If there is any experience it is incomplete.

V: You are store house of knowledge.

M: No. It is all empty. I talk what I do not know. You think it is my knowledge and appreciate it.

V: What spiritual practice do you recommend for me?

M: What you see, without deliberate seeing, with closed eyes, be there (meditate on it). It is called dark blue beauty (*Shyam Sunder*). It is the expanse of awareness (*Chidakash*). When you open the eyes, you see the great expanse of existence (*Mahadakash*).

V: Our ignorance is the cause of pride.

M: The primary illusion incarnates from spit. Who can be proud of that?

V: Is the state of *Parabrahman* full of knowledge?

M: It is the no-knowledge state, true and eternal. It is said, if the pranks of a beautiful young woman do not attract one, one is a *Jnani* or a beast.

V: Is a *Jnani* indifferent to what happens?

M: A *Jnani* leaves it to the nature to take care of His needs. What does the embryo do to feed itself? Who protects it and arranges a safe delivery? There is a better care in the no-knowing state than in the knowing. The deliberate action of an individual cannot be so perfect. These actions can be forgetful and inefficient. In scriptures it is written that a *Jnani* leaves it to destiny to do needful to His body. He has nothing to say about it. I equate *Prarabdha* (destiny) to *Sattva* quality which is responsible for beingness. A *Jnani*'s activities happen without the 'I Am' feeling.

We observe the five elements. Is there any mind?

V: No.

M: Stilll we observe conflict amongst them. Their activities happen without a mind. These elements do not know that they exist. When they combine to form *Sattva*, there is 'I amness' and mind in it. The development of forms and their activities happen spontaneously.

What is prior to mind and attention?

V: The sense of being.

M: Just as sour, pungent, hot are the qualities of food material, our sense of being or consciousness is also its quality or expression. Hence, the food material and the beingness are one only. The knower of consciousness is separate from it. Consciousness is the highest quality or stage of the (food) material, from where the Ultimate can be realized.

V: In spite of your passive witnessing, everything is going on smoothly here.

M: All that is a spontaneous happening. I am not a participant in it. It is like an embryo receiving everything that is needed.

V: What have we to understand from this?

M: One has to understand one's true form or nature.

V: Your visitors know you from your outward appearance and talk.

M: I am quite different from what appears and from what can be known. I am not this or anything of this. You see here the *Sattva* quality, which I am not. Your main obstacle in proper understanding is your attraction to your possessions, relatives and friends.

V: It is difficult to be free of them.

M: I work on you, like a sculptor on a stone. But his job seems to be easier than that of mine. A stone does not offer any resistance. As the artist works on it, it gets lighter and lighter. On the other hand my people seem to add on concepts, instead of becoming free of them.

V: While meditating what am I?

M: You are the formless consciousness. You know 'you are' because of the body; but you are not the body.

V: I become one with the witness.

M: You are the witness all the time. In the morning there was waking from the sleep state. The witnessing of waking happened to you and thereafter you witnessed the surroundings. All that you say as you see, you taste, you smell etc. is not your doing, but the happening of witnessing to you. You are prior to all experiences and actions. The witness never sleeps. The witness of waking and sleep states is beyond these states. What is operating now is the waking state. You listen to these talks and you are unable to speak; and the witness of these talks does not need to talk. The waking and sleep result from food material (*Sattva*); but the knower of these states is beyond *Sattva*. These states have rising and setting. The setting is considered as death by the people who are ignorant of the origin of waking i.e. consciousness. For a Sage there is no death, but bliss. Self knowledge is the end of fear and death.

V: How is a *Jnani* related to light?

M: There is no relation. Only its witnessing happens. The three ages *(Yugas)* have passed and the same have been witnessed. This witness is ever present and has no coming (birth) or going (death). Innumerable forms appear, remain and disappear; but the witness is only one and it remains forever, totally unaffected.

❧

December 30, 1979

THE MANIFESTATION
IS PURPOSELESS

Visitor: What is real surrender?

Maharaj: It is to forget one's name and form.

V: How does a Sadhaka (spiritual seeker) differ from an ordinary man?

M: An ordinary man relies on himself for his sustenance; whereas a Sadhaka relies on Guru or God for everything. A Sadhaka knows himself as consciousness and not the body.

V: How to overcome the fear of death?

M: The body identity must drop. The consciousness never dies. Live as consciousness and be fearless.

V: Are all our concepts due to Sattva?

M: Every concept including the first 'I Am' is due to Sattva.

V: If the whole world is in consciousness, where is Jnani?

M: He is out of the world. He is timeless and beyond being and non-being.

V: Can you bless me that only good will happen?

M: In reality, you are formless. What good or bad can happen to you? Everything is changing so fast, but your true nature remains unaffected. The best blessings are to realize what one is eternally. Only the changeless remains unaffected under all circumstances.

V: You talk less about individuals.

M: I talk about the collective relation of consciousness. When the five elements come together to form *Sattva*, various forms appear. One and the same consciousness operates through all forms. All individuals are imaginary. There is infinite and boundless consciousness, without any purpose. The vital breath also appears along with the consciousness.

V: The manifestation is purposeless, which is a very valuable information. May you live long to guide us.

M: I don't need to live even for a full day more. Life means trouble and it begins with waking every morning. You cannot avoid or even postpone running to the toilet. Taking care of your body's needs, you cannot expect lasting peace.

V: Is 'I amness' or consciousness our true nature?

M: No. It is our problem.

So far three ages (*Yugas*) have passed. They are *Satya*, *Treta* and *Dwapar*. The current is *Kali Yuga*. During this vast time is nature (*Nisarga*) affected in any way? *Nisarga* is not conscious, hence it is not at all affected.

The news 'I Am' is the cause of suffering. Where did it originate?

V: In the womb.

M: That news was the content of the Womb. My present experience of being alive and experiencing the world depends upon that news. That news is the foundation of this existence.

V: What was the condition, when the news was absent?

M: That was my true eternal state, which was untouched by several dissolutions of the universe.

V: How do people see visions of Gods and Sages?

M: Our consciousness has the power to appear in those forms. What is needed is the faith and a great urge to see these forms.

December 31, 1979

More The Greatness, More The Bondage

Maharaj: Lot of activity goes on in the womb for the transition from non-being to being. The non-being continues even after delivery of the infant upto over three years of its age.

Visitor: Some are lucky to become great in life.

M: More the greatness, more is the bondage. Even a small incident in one's life gets a big publicity all over the world. One has to be very careful all the time. There is freedom only in Self-knowledge.

V: A Guru gives initiation to his disciple. The Sanskrit word for initiation is *Anugraha*. What is its significance?

M: You have to accept (*graha*) your true identity from your Guru. He tells, you are atomic (*anu*) consciousness. The disciples continue to have their body identity. But that is not accepting initiation.

V: From what age does accumulation of knowledge begin?

M: For accumulating knowledge the child must first know that it exists. It is self-knowledge (not Self-knowledge). That

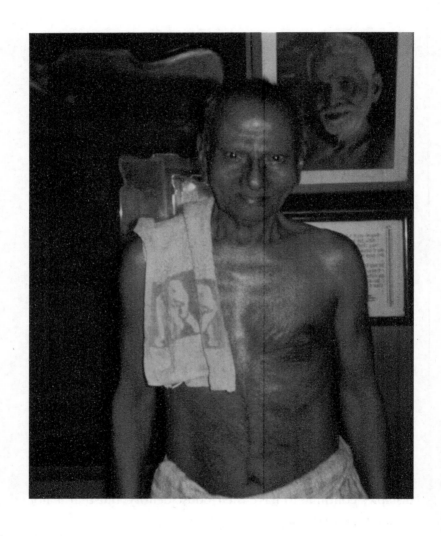

happens around three to five years age. It is when the child starts recognising its mother. The collection of ignorance begins thereafter.

V: If the child is taught that it is not the body but the consciousness or Self, will it realize the Self faster?

M: The child will not understand it. It will remember the words and repeat them like a parrot. That will not help in any way. At the end of the life span, all the accumulated knowledge vanishes. The strength also becomes less and less day by day, and at the end, no energy is left even to lift a feeding spoon.

V: We, ignorant people, always have family thoughts, worldly thoughts flowing. What about a *Jnani*'s thoughts?

M: Those thoughts are absent here. In your case, there are hopes, desires and cravings. Your thought flow is because of them. In case of a *Jnani*, the hopes etc. don't die, but they are fulfilled spontaneously.

V: I see a lot of exaggeration in scriptures.

M: In the epic *Mahabharat* it is written in Krishna's kingdom there lived his followers called Yadavas, totalling fifty six crores in number. What is current population of India?

V: Around seventy crores.

M: In a small part of the present Gujarat State how could so many Yadavas have lived comfortably? We read many such things. What is true and what is false in it?

V: What does a Sadguru do to His disciple?

M: He ends his 'I amness' and the unreal existence. In the infinite and boundless, unhappiness cannot remain.

V: What is the significance of Godess Laxmi serving God Narayan.

M: Here consciousness is Narayan and our attention (*Lax*)

I Am (*mi*) serves it. In the ocean of consciousness, your sense of being is so minute. When it goes, it is all one consciousness.

V: Ram was *Parabrahman*. Was He never ignorant?

M: When He was young, He was like you. The teachings of His Guru Sage Vasistha changed Him.

V: What is real knowledge?

M: It is to know that I am neither the *Sattva* food body nor its quality of consciousness.

V: Do you believe in miracles?

M: A minute sphere of consciousness has become the great expanse of existence – the universe of matter and energy. Is it not a miracle?

The size of our earth is so minute as compared to the total existence. A small particle of *Sattva* on this earth has consciousness, which contains the whole existence. What more do you need to believe in miracles?

January 1, 1980

You Look For Simple Truth - Made Difficult

Visitor: What do I gain by Self-knowledge?

Maharaj: The idea of profit and loss is a sign of the body identity and they apply to an individual. With Self-knowledge these concepts don't remain. When the individual is no more, to whose account will you put the profit or loss? In the formless there are no separate accounts to register profit or loss. It is all one account or no account. If you are looking for profit, this (Nisargadatta Ashram) is a wrong place for you.

V: The rich are very careful to book maximum profit.

M: There life is a needless struggle. Others in the family have no work. Their job is to take their dog out for a walk. I have seen a Parsi gentleman sleeping with his dog on his stomach. Now, forget about profit and loss, tell me what is the use of your beingness when you lose your individuality?

V: No use. Then, there will be no happiness or unhappiness.

M: All rivers join the sea. Also, all gutters empty into it. How does it affect the sea? Similarly, a Sage is unaffected by the good or bad of the world.

Our knowledge 'I Am' (consciousness) is a borrowed knowledge. It is bound to leave. Your state a hundred years back was similar to your present deep sleep state. There were no thoughts in both these states. Hence, try to remain without thoughts (meditation) as long as possible. You will get true knowledge thereby.

V: What is true knowledge?

M: You experience the world due to your waking and sleep states. When you know the "why and how" of these states, it is an end of all your search for knowledge.

V: Where will I go at the end of this life?

M: You know that you did not come here from anywhere. You appeared unknowingly and almost suddenly. You will also disappear in the same way. If you are bold enough, you will be able to say 'good-bye' at the end.

Just as your world began with your consciousness, it will also end with the separation of consciousness. Your being and the world are one only. Just like the sun and its light, you are the sun and the world is your light.

You have not done anything for the appearance of your consciousness. When it separates (death) you cannot stop it. Also, it is not in your hands to get rid of it.

V: Is knowingness same as consciousness or beingness?

M: Yes. That is your main capital. You have to think over knowingness, who comes to know and how it has happened. Whatever is seen in the knowingness is the transformation of knowingness. Whatever you know is because of your knowingness. What can you know without it? People take interest in what they know and not in knowingness itself. When you come to know the secret of this knowingness (its origin) you will attain fullness and all your needs will come to an end. Remember that you are neither the known nor the knowingness, but are the knower of knowingness. Today I am talking about knowingness and I will not leave the subject. I will not allow you to come to the body level. You go to dramas and movies, but I don't go, why? Because you love your knowingness, but you cannot tolerate it without doing something or the other. In order to be comfortable, you have to keep your knowingness busy. In my case, I do not need my knowingness. Also, it is not a problem for me. I am not the knowingness but its knower.

Before the appearance of this knowingness was there any need to exist or to continue to exist? Just as knowingness has a beginning, it has also an end. It is as if a convict is sentenced to death by hanging. Only the date is not yet fixed.

V: How are the five elements related to knowingness?

M: They are the content of knowingness and cannot exist independent of knowingness.

V: If the Truth is so simple, how are we still in concepts?

M: That is your own contribution. My job is to tell you 'what is'. It is left to you, how you understand it or misunderstand it. You look for simple Truth made difficult. Hence, you cannot help wrapping It up in your own concepts. You can be excused for your mistakes, but there are so called Gurus, who are not much different from you. Their most fond concept is their *Brahman*. They are eager to share their great findings with their disciples. A Guru's greatness is not measured by his realization of the Self, but by his number of followers. More the followers, bigger is the Guru. I don't blame them (Gurus), as they do not know that they are still ignorant. Their hopes, desires and cravings are a measure of their ignorance. How can the formless have any hopes or desires?

V: Why is it difficult to transcend all concepts?

M: It is your liking and love for these concepts, that binds you. You promote your concepts to the stature of *Brahman*.

V: Why is there so much love for existence?

M: In case of every living being what is born is 'I love', the love to exist. This is a sign of ignorance. The precious life is used by human beings to pass time somehow. The value of life is known only at the end, when the last few days or hours are left. The doctors are requested to keep the patient alive at any cost. This 'I love' vanishes when the secret of transition from the 'no knowing' to 'knowing' is known. A Sage has no 'I love'. Hence, He does not need body-guards. He (or she) drops the body voluntarily which is termed *Yogic Maha Samadhi* or leaves it to nature or *Prarabdha* (destiny). What was your name, form and quality a hundred years back?

V: Nothing.

M: The same is now witnessing innumerable names, forms and qualities.

V: Our thoughts are about weather, rising prices, politics etc. What are your thought like?

M: I think about the content of scriptures like *Mahabharat* etc. There is a description about the birth of Pandawas and Kauravas. I wonder how far they are true! There is conception from non-existing males. Is that possible? etc. What is the reality of this great world of ours? The only reply I get is that it is all an imagination.

People read *Bhagavad Gita* to know what were Arjuna's doubts and how did Shri Krishna help him. I tell the readers that Krishna is referring to their own problems, and is trying to help them in life. Can the reader know what he is and how? The author of *Mahabharat*, Sage Vyas, has made Arjuna only an instrumental in awakening the readers to their true nature.

V: Words play an important role in our lives.

M: With the infant's form in front of them, the parents name it as per the word that occurs to them. Every name has its meaning. A man acts as per the meaning of thoughts that occur to him. Can one expect proper action by uttering meaningless words?

M: Your day begins with actions as per the thoughts that come after waking in the morning. Witnessing of the whole day happens to the waking state that begins in the morning. For realizing your true nature you must stabilize in the state prior to waking. There are no words in that state. Your experience of the world and your activities begin after the appearance of the news 'I Am'. Before that what was there? Were you a man or a woman?

V: Nothing.

M: The first silent words are 'I Am'. Your day begins with words and words every morning. Your actions depend upon them. You call them thoughts. Your words combine to form a sentence. Then only you are able to ask your question. Which soap do you use to clean your ignorance?

V: Such a soap is not available.

M: That is a soap of knowledge, which you receive from a Guru. When the heard and read ignorance is cleansed along with your own imagined concepts, pure Self-knowledge remains. The Self is permanent and ever ready, without which the temporary ignorance cannot exist. But the ignorance is so prominent that the Self appears to be imaginary and temporary. The ignorance looks very ancient and well established. The worst part of the ignorance is the body identity, which is the most difficult to eradicate. The ignorance, including the body identity, can be less or more, but the Self is ever full and complete. With true knowledge the ignorance gets liberation, but not the Self, which is never in bondage.

V: What happens when the body identity is lost?

M: Then you know that you are the entire manifestation – vast and unlimited.

V: You once said "I am awake" is also a concept. How?

M: Your true nature is beyond waking, sleep and knowingness and ever awake. From that angle to say "I am awake" is odd and a concept.

V: How do we accept as true, whatever we hear?

M: All your knowledge is based on hearsay only. You find it convenient to go with the majority. Whatsoever ninety nine people believe, the hundredth man also easily believes. Birth is nobody's own experience. Still it is taken as the truth.

V: What is the solution to this?

M: All hearsay knowledge should get dropped. Don't entertain public opinion. What we are, should be our own knowledge. All religions are based on hearsay and the Self is unaffected and independent of it.

To which religion do sleep and consciousness belong?

V: To no religion.

M: Our birth means the appearance of waking, sleep and consciousness. The combination of these three gives rise to the memory 'I Am', which has accepted religions as per the traditions.

V: Are sin or religious merit real or imagination?

M: If they were real, you would have known them even in deep sleep or also a hundred years back. In these two states you were perfectly pure in all respects. All your problems are due to the memory 'I Am' and the body identity. In the absence of the body identity, there is no birth, no death and no bondage. Taking yourself as the body, what you collect in this world is all ignorance only. You take yourself as a man or a woman because of the body form, which is also ignorance.

V: After ignoring all hearsay, what should one do?

M: One should abide in one's own Self. Without asking anybody you can be sure of only one thing that is your sense of being, your consciousness. This is your main capital. Be with it. Meditate on it and it will tell you the Truth. That will not be a hearsay but your own direct knowledge. When the body is forgotten, there is peace and purity.

V: How long should I meditate?

M: Until you forget that you are meditating. This will be possible by practise, provided you are earnest. Otherwise, you may meditate for one or two hours between 3am to 6am every morning, or as is convenient.

V: What is the cause of fear?

M: Was there any fear before getting concepts from others?

V: No.

M: Don't accept others' concepts and be fearless. What is your main demand?

V: That I should remain alive.

M: All your activities are to remain alive. "I am alive" is a concept from the standpoint of your true nature, which never dies. Hence, "I am alive" concept must get dropped.

V: What is Moola Maya (illusion)?

M: In your true Eternal state, the sense of being was absent. Its appearance is the most attractive. That is Moola Maya. The sense of being is timebound and not indefinite.

V: How can a man attain *Brahman*?

M: When we talk of a man or a woman, it is understood that they have a body identity. Such a person cannot know *Brahman*.

V: What is actually seen how can it be untrue?

M: You see a dream. Is it true? In the waking state also you see, but it is not much different from a dream. Your sense of being always contains various scenes full of objects. You cannot separate the scene from the sense of being. The sense of being is the *Sattva* quality of food essence. When *Sattva* is not, there is nothing.

January 2, 1980

WHO COMES TO KNOW THAT ALL EXISTENCE IS FALSE?

Visitor: How do you say that all our knowledge is hearsay?

Maharaj: What is your own knowledge? Did you know that you were a girl?

V: No.

M: A drop knows about the ocean; but when it becomes one with the ocean, it does not know that it is an ocean.

V: Are there any duties after Self knowledge?

M: Then, you are free of all bondages and duties. All your normal activities and duties are to protect yourself and to preserve your 'I love'. For a *Jnani*, there is no 'I love', and therefore no question of protecting it.

V: Why is God not a need of all?

M: You need water only when you are thirsty.

V: Is a *Jnani* free to do anything?

M: If you are working in a company, you have to follow their rules and regulations. Your expectation of a regular income is your bondage. A *Jnani* is free of all expectations including the need to exist. Hence, He is really free. For Him life is a play (leela). Still His utterances and actions are in tune with the Absolute. A *Jnani* does not need to follow any religion. Most of the religions have begun from *Jnanis*. One who has seen oneself properly, His self surrender is complete. This has happened here (in my case) and now there is no need for any religion. This talk, which is going on now, is the quality of food material (*Sattva*). A *Jnani* is always the knower of consciousness and is separate from it. He makes use of consciousness as an instrument, to communicate.

V: Why are half baked Gurus not coming here to get their baking completed?

M: Their pose is coming in their way. They are Sadhus, Mahatmas, Sants or Rishis. They have their own following. They cannot sacrifice all that for Self knowledge. Here (in my case) there is no pose. It is all space like and open. In our path of devotion (*Bhakti Marga*) initially a disciple has to take himself as *Brahman*. After attaining It, there is no need to repeat "I am *Brahman*". One lives as *Brahman*, which is real *Brahmacharya* (Celibacy), without any announcement or publicity. That is the picture of fullness and end of all desires. How were Ramkrishna Paramahansa, Shirdi Sai Baba, Nityanand, Ramana Maharshi and other great Sages? The concepts of profit and loss have no place there, including all bondages, which are reserved for the half baked.

People come here with their own ideas and innocently try to involve me. Once a woman came here with some *prasad*, after visiting Pandharpur. She wanted me to take advantage of her visit to Vithoba. I told her to keep the *prasad* there, so that I could consume it later on.

Another women invited me to accompany them on a visit

to one thousand year old Babaji, who had come to Bombay (Mumbai) on a visit. I told them to visit him and later tell me about their meeting.

V: A seeker, without a pose, can pursue his meditation without any disturbance.

M: Suppose there is a poor and deserving girl, who needs your help. You take the pose of her father. Then you are bound to spend your time, money and energy for her. Sadhus are so busy in their worldly activities that they have no time for meditation. They have no time even to think about their Guru's teachings. Their major time is spent in going from place to place, giving lectures. They remain on the intellectual level and cannot go beyond it. For some time, I had also taken a small pose. I saw its disadvantages and gave it up. Now, there is no pose here.

V: What about the knowledge of the Eternal Self?

M: This consciousness is not going to remain for a long time. While it lasts, one must know one's state, then the consciousness will be no more. For that knowledge, one cannot wait for the departure of the consciousness.

V: If a *Jnani* is without a pose. He is free of all responsibilities.

M: On the other hand His responsibility increases. He has to take care of the whole universe. But there is no involvement in it. Beyond all concepts, there is total freedom.

V: When you talk to us, what do you take us to be?

M: I talk to the unborn principle, but you hear me as a born being. The consciousness is *Atma* and *Paramatma* is the unborn Principle.

Before coming here you were living with the 'I-am-the body idea. How are you going to live now?

V: After losing the body identity. I will live as the consciousness. Can consciousness know *Parabrahman?*

M: No. But *Parabrahman* knows the consciousness, although there is no need to know it.

You love watching T.V. What is there?

V: It is all an illusion.

M: If the actors are not alive, are they dead? If dead, you should be able to see corpses there. Who is watching the T.V.?

V: They are also an illusion.

M: One who says that there was dissolution of the Universe, but I did not even notice it, is he a knower or ignorant?

(Silence.)

M: A fisherman spreads his net to catch fish. Whatever gets caught in the net, is his catch. Similarly, whatever comes in the grasp of your intellect is your knowledge. When you hear the word *Parabrahman*, it is not understood by your intellect. You do not understand by your intellect. You can hear the word, but cannot have any taste or experience of it. You do not understand that which is prior to your being, during your being and also after your being. In fact it is *Parabrahman* which understands and not you. It is never an object, but always the Subject.

The only key you have to *Parabrahman* is your consciousness. Purify it by chanting the *Mantra* (*Mahavakya*) given by Sadguru. *Parabrahman* is already there waiting, when the false is seen as false.

V: If all existence is spontaneous, what is my duty?

M: You have to only know that 'you' are not in it.

V: Who comes to know that all existence is false?

M: Whoever knows is also false.

V: One who is trying to know the Truth, how can he be unreal?

M: He is unreal. That is a fact.

V: What is the motive for searching for the Truth?

M: Restlessness.

V: What is the cause of restlessness?

M: Wrong identity. To take yourself as that which you are not, is the cause of all the confusion and trouble.

V: Then, what is the solution to this problem?

M: To remember Sadguru's words round the clock. Thereby, the Truth will manifest in you. Shri Krishna tells this to Arjuna, "Surrender to me alone, completely."

Everyone gets a call from within to know the Truth. But it is never heard by most of the people.

Now, I ask you what is the expenditure of the whole world and after debiting it, what is the credit balance?

(Silence.)

V: What is real surrender?

M: It is dropping the "I-am-the body" idea.

V: Why are devotees told to surrender to Ram, Krishna etc.

M: That is in the initial stages, when it is difficult to drop the body identity, for the beginners.

V: What is the cause of unhappiness and pain?

M: Your sticking to the body as 'I Am'.

❧

January 3, 1980

What You Accept In Full Faith, Happens

&

Maharaj: All your world is the creation of your beingness. You may find this difficult to accept; but what about your dream world?

Visitor: The false waking in deep sleep results in the appearance of the dream world. There is no God needed to create it.

M: What applies to the dream state also applies to the waking. Your consciousness is nothing less than God. Have you realized your greatness?

V: I am a pitiable mortal; struggling to know the Truth.

M: What are you without your body form? I am referring to that. At night you cannot see objects in darkness. When the Sun rises, the same objects become visible. Similarly, in deep sleep the objects are invisible. Your waking is the Sun in whose light the world becomes visible.

If you limit yourself to your body, you suffer. Without the body you are invisible. Give your attention to it. Even in complete darkness, you know that you are. Hold it. Meditate on it.

V: We never question the reality of any experience in waking or in a dream, while it lasts.

M: All experiences accompany your sense of being. When the sense of being is absent, as in deep sleep, there is nothing. You see bright afternoon sunlight even on a moonless midnight. You call it a dream.

V: How can meditation help to wake up from this dream? We dream even while waking.

M: When you meditate properly on your consciousness, in due course, you will yourself see in it all the five elements, three qualities and the *Prakriti* and *Purusha*. For complete peace and happiness you will have to propitiate your consciousness, by meditating on it. Thereafter, you will be so full in all respects that there will be no need for anything.

V: If death is a myth, how can a *Jnani* die?

M: If a *Jnani* says that he is going to die, he cannot be a *Jnani*.

V: We worship Gods like Rama and Krishna. Were they human beings like us? If so, we can also strive to be like them.

M: They were just like you. If you call them incarnations, you are also incarnations. That is the greatness of consciousness in human form. The only requirement is its proper use under the guidance of a Sadguru.

V: Although the Truth is so simple, some people undergo great hardships for Self-realization.

M: If a disciple does not have any doubt about his Sadguru's teachings, he realizes the highest in no time. But such is a rare case. Full faith in one's consciousness works wonders. In the initial stages, people are told to chant *Mantra* and do *bhajans*. They also achieve, but after a long time.

V: Can you suggest to me some short cut, for regular practise?

M: During day time you are busy with so many activities. At least while going to bed at night say the following, "My body is made of the five elements. If I am not the elements, how can I be the body? My *prana* (vital breath) is formless. My consciousness and mind are also formless. How can I be limited to a small form? I am infinite and boundless. I am ever existing. How can I be born? Hence, I cannot have any death also. I am the Eternal ever existing Principle". With your insistence, necessary changes will take place in you during sleep and your spiritual progress will be easier and faster. What you accept in full faith, happens in reality.

V: The other day I saw you curing a serious illness of a disciple.

M: His condition was really bad. I told him, "There is nothing wrong with you. You are absolutely fine". He had full faith in me and had come to me as the last hope. He accepted my words as the absolute truth. My job was to create confidence in him. What worked was his own faith. He was free of his sickness in a short time. Some people give me credit for the miracles that happen. In fact I don't do anything. If I were responsible for doing miracles. I could have done them even in the absence of faith in me. All don't benefit by coming here.

V: If *Atma* is one in all, it should be easier to have full faith in the Sadguru.

M: Atma is one, the world *Atma* (*Jagadatma*) or the universal *Atma* (*Vishwatma*) which finally merges into the attributeless *Paramatma*. But the faith one has in the Sadguru differs from disciple to disciple. One is free not to have faith and suffer accordingly. In one of our *bhajans*, it is said that even God is bound to help a disciple who has full faith that his Sadguru is *Parabrahman*.

V: Although I am not this body, it is more prominent than the consciousness, which is invisible.

M: Never bring the consciousness to the level of the body. Consciousness or *Atma* appear to be restricted to the body, which is never so. It is everywhere, infinite and boundless. You come to know that you exist because of your body. But you are not the body.

You agree that space is limitless. Now, space and the other four elements, originate from consciousness. It means consciousness is bigger than space. Then, how can consciousness get restricted to the body. It is also infinite and boundless.

V: After Self-knowledge, whom should I consult in case of any doubts?

M: Existence of any doubt indicates lack of Self-knowledge. The concept "I have Self-knowledge" should also drop.

V: As a beginner can you tell me where should I begin my Self-enquiry?

M: A hundred years back you were not knowing your existence. Even your body appeared without your knowledge. Your existence was in a no-knowing state. Now, you know that you are. You must know the transition from the no-knowing state to the knowing state. What is the reason for this transition and how? Your mind cannot help to find out, as it was absent during this transition. It came later on. It is enough if it does not disturb you during your enquiry. Without it, you will have a nice, deep meditation in which all your doubts will be cleared.

Your Self-enquiry has started because of the body. When there was no body you did not know your existence. Hence, there was no need for any enquiry. As long as the body is there, you have to complete your Self-enquiry. Meditation is the key to the solution of this spiritual riddle.

V: What is the ultimate finding of spirituality?

M: Your sense of being (consciousness) is the quality of the essence of food you eat. Somebody comes to know that he is. Who is he? He must be present prior to knowing his presence. Then why did he not know when the body was born? Then also the food essence was ready, but it was raw. In a raw mango there is no sweetness. The sweetness comes when the mango ripens after some months. Similarly, the knowingness appeared three to five years after the birth of the body. What is the most important thing in your life?

V: My sense of being.

M: What is there without it? Nothing. Hence, that is your capital. That is everything for you and it is your key to Self-knowledge. Meditate on it. When your consiousness is propitiated, it will be an end to all your doubts and questions. Then, you will have lasting happiness.

V: I exist and have my own ideas about myself. How long will they last?

M: As long as your body is intact. Here (in my case) there are no ideas. "What is" cannot be described as like this or like that. It is unlike anything else. I do not find myself useful to the world, still I Am. My physical existence is this news 'I Am' in the body. It has come uncalled for and it can go any moment. How much importance should I give to this unreliable physical existence? My real existence is independent of this body. I existed when the body was not. Even now I exist independent of the body. The body is not required for my existence, only my news 'I Am' needs it. Without the body I do not know 'I Am'. In future also I will be there without this body and without the news 'I Am'.

V: The appearance of beingness is like waking up from deep sleep.

M: One, who was without any attributes and was beyond consciousness, suddenly became conscious. It is not someone coming from somewhere, but it is only becoming conscious of one's existence. From the no 'news state', the news 'I Am' appeared.

V: Is there any permanent experience?

M: All your experiences depend upon your sense of being, which itself is impermanent. Only the no-experience state is permanent.

V: What remains to be done after meeting a Sage?

M: Try to remember his words all the time and remain as per His words, as much as possible. That will keep you closer to Reality. You must look at yourself and not at God or others.

❦

January 4, 1980

A Sage Is Rich Without Possessions

ふん

Visitor: Our bodies have value because of the consciousness. What is the value of consciousness?

Maharaj: Consciousness is God. Who is there other than itself (consciousness) to evaluate? An advanced seeker says, I am the formless consciousness.

V: Who is a sinner?

M: The consciousness never dies but only separates from the body. One who says "I am dying" is a sinner.

V: We receive so much from our Sadguru. What value do we give to it?

M: A millionaire had a loss of memory and he was begging on a pavement. A friend of his recognised him and offered all help to bring him back on track. He told him his worth and named the bank in which he had millions. Can you expect that beggar to continue his stay on the pavement? In spirituality it is happening like that. I tell you what you are. You are not a pitiable mortal, but you are a formless, deathless, infinite and boundless Principle. If you continue to hold on to your old identity, what can I do?

V: A gain of a few thousand rupees is of more importance to us than the knowledge of our true nature. We do not know its importance. We understand material gain but not spiritual.

M: Everything becomes visible because of your consciousness, which itself is invisible. The wise know the importance of consciousness now, but the dull have to wait until their end. How much one has to spend in order to keep a patient alive? Many a times, money cannot help at all.

V: The ignorant live as men and also die as men. What does the Sadguru do?

M: He waters the seed of *Brahman* in you and in due course there will be fully grown tree of *Brahman* in you.

You are always the *Chaitanya Brahman* on which there is an illusory appearance of a human being.

Sadguru's help is required to know and realize our true being.

V: What was my last birth?

M: This question arises from the body identity, which is made of earth, water, fire, air and space. I will answer your question after you tell me what was the last birth of the content of earth in you. Also what was the last birth of the water in you. Similarly, tell me the last birth of fire, air and space in you. Just as the five elements have no birth, the body made up of these five elements also has no birth.

V: All our knowledge in this field is ignorance only.

Why are Sadgurus so rare?

M: Their number is as per the demand. Are there many seekers for Self-knowledge? There are mostly self-seekers and rarely

Self-seekers. One, who is beyond all needs, welcomes true seekers. A Sage poses as an ignorant man or even as mad, in order to keep the wrong people away. The earnest seekers find no difficulty in meeting the right man.

V: The rich and powerful people can help to give publicity.

M: But who needs publicity? The need for consciousness has ended here, hence what can one gain through consciousness? A Sage is rich without possessions. Your desires and wants make you poor or rich. You can come across rich beggars, but a desireless poor is rare to find.

V: Where should I search for the Truth?

M: It is within you and not outside. All the outer search should end so that the inner search gets concentrated. Once the Truth is located within, it will be everywhere for you.

V: How to get rid of the "I am the body" idea?

M: You never say that you are the food that you eat. It should be very clear to you that this body is nothing but food material. Your consciousness eats this body during fasting. With constant reminding the wrong idea will get dropped.

You are formless, but your body is the nearest form because of which you know 'you are'. Because of this proximity, you are holding this body as your form.

V: Do I exist without the body?

M: Yes, but that existence is without "I". That was your existence a hundred years back. That is Eternal existence. There is no 'I' or ' you' in It.

It is all one (alone). The same *Atma* is in all living beings. Only their forms differ and they are named accordingly.

V: If I search within, will I get liberated?

M: All your concepts will be liberated. Without them, you

are already free, without needing any liberation. To be free of concepts is to have real knowledge of what life is.

V: Why are Sages mostly silent and talk to only a few?

M: Why was Jesus crucified and Mansoor killed by his fellow Muslims? Only a few can hear Truth patiently and digest it. The Truth cannot be given to all and sundry. The masses are destined to remain in ignorance only. Hence, the Sages impart knowledge only to a chosen few.

In my case, both God and devotee have vanished and here I am. What do you understand by it? At this stage, I feel it is improper for people to visit and listen to me. Brahma is the creator God of the Hindu Trinity. The last day and date is said to be noted on the forehead of every living being. But who writes the last day on the forehead of Brahma himself? Shiva or Shankar is the great destroyer responsible for all dissolutions. Who writes the last day on Shankar's forehead? All these riddles have been solved here (in my case). All secrecies have found their liberation in this place. With all that, my true nature has remained unaffected and intact. I cannot produce a witness to confirm all this and there is no need for it.

If somebody asks whether I have a mind and what are my thoughts are like, the above sentences will give him some idea.

V: All forms should be eternal, as *Atma* is the only Truth.

M: All forms are due to the five elements, which are not eternal. Your true nature is bodiless and independent of the five elements. Hence, It is Eternal. You know the world because of consciousness, which you are not. The consciousness is your instrument and you are its user and knower.

Without consciousness what do you witness?

V: Nothing.

M: Hence forget the body and be with the consciousness alone, as much as possible and as long as possible. That is called meditation. Thereafter you will see the world as the play of your consciousness.

Without knowing the origin of consciousness, whatever you may do, it will never give you real, lasting happiness. The real knowledge frees you from illusory bondage.

V: I love to exist. Consciousness is a blessing for me.

M: Then, why do you sleep? Try to live without sleep.

V: Regular sleep is a must

M: Sleep is forgetting consciousness and it is a must for survival. What must be forgotten regularly cannot be a blessing. Even when awake you have to forget consciousness by some mental or physical activity. Both food and sleep are necessary for survival.

V: What about the individual soul (*jeeva*), world and *Brahman*?

M: Witnessing happens due to consciousness and there are the individual soul, world and *Brahman*. Without consciousness there is nothing and no witnessing. 'I Am' is a concept and all is its creation. Your sense of being is the soul (Sarvatma) of all existence.

V: What about your 'I Am'.

M: When investigated, it vanished.

V: You do not advise your disciples to observe any restrictions.

M: For me this existence is the child of a barren woman. What difference will it make if the child behaves any way? Sage Ramdas had told his disciples that they were asking him to give details about something, which had never happened.

V: Have you met Sri J. Krishnamurti?

M: If I happen to meet Him, what should I talk? There may be some exchange of words, but not of knowledge. Here also It is the same. I have had the conviction whether I am there or not (whether I really exist or not).

January 5, 1980

EXISTENCE IS JUST AN APPEARANCE

⁑

Maharaj: The same child consciousness continues throughout the life upto the last day. So many changes take place in the body and around it, but the child consciousness remains the same. The witnessing of the whole life happens to the child consciousness. When it separates from the body, it is all over.

Visitor: How do concepts affect the child consciousness?

M: The flow of concepts continues throughout the life. New concepts come, they remain for some time and go, but the child consciousness remains unchanged. What we call as death is the setting of the child consciousness. Till then the seed quality is wet. When it gets dried up, the child consciousness sets. All human activities are during the period from rising to setting of the child consciousness.

V: Is it possible to be free of thoughts indefinitely?

M: No. It can be only for a duration. As long as there is consciousness and breathing, thoughts will arise. You call it mind. You are disturbed by thoughts. The question is who controls whom? You control your mind or your mind controls you? Your mind is like an elephant which takes you for a ride. In the case of a Sage the mind is like a fly taking a ride on the elephant.

V: If we are *Brahman* in reality, it should be easy for us to hold our Self.

M: It is easier to hold something, which you are not.

M: How can you hold yourself and which part will you hold? You are It (Self) all the time and any action of yourself is going away from It.

V: If we are one with the world, why this multiplicity?

M: It is because your devotion to your Sadguru is not complete.

V: Is there really a third eye in the forehead?

M: The third eye is of knowledge, which you receive from your Sadguru.

V: Is a Sage free even when he utters irrelevant words in high fever?

M: One who is liberated and free is always so in all circumstances.

V: We see old people busy in their worldly activities till their end.

M: They have fear of death and their lives are just an effort to forget it. A spiritual seeker lives only to realize his immortality.

V: Why to sacrifice comforts and entertainment for Self realization, which may not materialise?

M: You are consciousness and all the creation are your forms and your births. Avoiding spirituality is nothing new to you, but that is your normal practice. Then, why not opt for the higher at least in this life? The human potential is to be God and it is worth trying for, at any cost.

V: Your grace is always in action and many a times, we are respected for no apparent reason.

M: Always have a feeling that through you, people are respecting your Sadguru.

V: Should I continue my *bhajans* even after Self-knowledge?

M: Yes. That will enhance or maintain your worthiness and save you from a fall.

V: Is life worth living?

M: The best use is to continue your devotion to Sadguru.

V: How far can I progress without full faith in Sadguru?

M: Without it, you cannot realize your unity with the Absolute.

V: In life we have so many Gurus. What is Sadguru's greatness?

M: When you construct a temple, many play their part in completing the work. The architect, civil engineer, construction workers and coolies play their part. The sculptor has also to do important work. But the final installation and doing the rite of bringing life into the image is done only by the *brahmin* priest. Similarly, only a Sadguru can awaken you to your true Self.

V: Has spirituality lost its importance in this modern age?

M: Your technology has advanced but your problems and suffering have not changed. Formerly, you had problems with your bullock carts. Now, they are with your cars and jets. Your jealousy, hatred, anger and sorrow are the same as before. You will laugh at a person who is travelling in a train or bus with a suitcase on his head. Even now you are used to living life with imaginary problems and fears. Short-lived gains and happiness demand great efforts, which you don't hesitate to put in. But real ease, lasting peace and happiness, and natural spontaneity are unknown to you all. A rare one is an exception to this. Turning to spirituality demands wisdom to understand the limitations of your worldly life. A very few have it and they are the salt of the earth. Others live to struggle and die.

The modern age has enabled man to have enough, but of no use for lasting peace and happiness. Hence, more and more people are turning to spirituality to try its worth.

V: Why are Sages unperturbed by disturbing events?

M: The Sages are nothing short of *Parabrahman*, which was totally unaffected even during the several dissolutions of the universe. An ocean is unaffected by a few drops of rain falling into it here and there. The Sages don't do anything but the people near them do benefit and their problems get solved. Sage Ramdas was the Guru of Chhatrapati Shivaji Maharaj who struggled to save Hindustan from total destruction under Muslim invasions and misrule.

V: Most people lack in devotion.

M: Every living being has devotion to be alive. No effort is spared to remain alive.

V: How can I be sure that I am on the right track in spirituality?

M: When you stay put in consciousness without using it for other activities.

V: My mind disturbs me during meditation.

M: Be a real devotee of a Sadguru. Then you will go beyond your mind.

V: I agree that the dream world is false, but what about the waking world?

M: Both are the content of your consciousness and time bound. How can they be true?

V: I want to get rid of this love to live.

M: Then know your Self.

V: What is real worship of God?

M: The real worship is to know that in your pure form you are God.

V: It is said that *Paramatma* is without the sense of being or the 'I Am' knowledge.

M: The news 'I Am' is absent in the formless *Paramatma*. That news is the quality of the body form. The news appeared because of the body and it mistook the body as its form. The world exists in consciousness and the consciousness in *Paramatma*.

❧

GLOSSARY

Ajnana   Ignorance
Ananda   Bliss
Anugraha   Initiation
Atma   The Self
Atmananda   Bliss of the Self
Atmaprakash   Light of the Self

Beingness   Consciousness, I Amness,
                        Knowledge I am or you are
Bhaktimarga   The path of devotion
Bodhisattva   The essence of intelligence
Brahmasutra   Cosmic mind

Child consciousness   Pure consciousness of a child
Chaitanya   Consciousness
Chakras   Plexus (Muladhar,
                        Swadhishthan, Manipur,
                        Anahat, Vishuddha, Ajna)
Chidananda   Consciousness – bliss

Dhyan   Meditation

Guna   Quality
Hiranyagarbha   Cosmic intelligence,
                        Universal consciousness

Ishwara   God

Jagadatma	The Supreme Being
Jagruti	Waking state
Jnana	Knowledge, consciousness
Jnani	A Sage
Kailas	The abode of Shiva or Shankar
Karma	Action
Mahasamadhi	Dropping of body by a Sage
Maya	Illusion, The illusive power of Brahman
Maha-Tatwa	The Great Reality, Supreme Consciousness
MoolMaya	Primary illusion
Mumukshu	Spiritual seeker
Nirguna	Unmanifest, Attributeless
Nisarga	Nature
Nirvikalpa	Without modifications of mind
Paramatma	The Supreme Reality
Paramananda	Supreme bliss
Peetambara	Yellow coloured silk dhoti
Prakruti	Cosmic Substance
Pranayam	The Yogic control of breath
Parabrahma	The Supreme Reality
Prarabdha	Destiny. Stored effects of past actions
Purusha	The cosmic spirit
Rajas	One of the three qualities, restlessness

Saguna Bhakti	Idol worship. (Saguna means the manifested)
Sarvatma	The Self in all, the Cosmic Self
Sahaja State	The most natural state (of a Jnani)
Sahajawastha	Natural state
Sahaja Yoga	The easy Yoga
Sadananda	Always in bliss
Samadhi	Oneness with Self
Sadhaka	Advanced (earnest) seeker
Satchidananda	Existence, consciousness, bliss
Sattva	True essence, one of the three qualities
Shaktipat	A type of spiritual Yoga
Siddha	A perfected being
Swavishaya	Meditation on Self
Tamas	One of the three qualities, claiming doership
That-ananda / This-ananda	Joining the suffix of ananda to any word like this or that forms name of an ochre robed
Vaikuntha	Abode of Vishnu
Vasudeva	One of the names of Krishna
Veda	Ancient Hindu scripture
Videhi	One in a bodiless state
Vijnana	Principle of pure intelligence, Beyond knowledge (Jnana)
Vishwambhara	Universal God
Vishwatma	The Supreme Being